Top 10 Traits *of*

Silicon Valley

Dynamos

*Inspiring Stories and Great Ideas for
Achieving Success in Your Life*

Joan Clout-Kruse

DUNHILL
PUBLISHING

Published by Dunhill Publishing
18340 Sonoma Highway Sonoma, California 95476

Printed and bound in the United States of America.

Clout-Kruse, Joan
Top10 traits of Silicon Valley Dynamos: Inspiring Stories and Great Ideas
for Achieving Success in Your Life / by Joan Clout-Kruse—1st ed.
p.cm.
Includes bibliographical references.
LCCN: 2001130386
ISBN: 1-931501-14-9

1.Success 2.Success in Business. 3.Successful people—California—
Santa Clara Valley (Santa Clara County) I. Title.
BF637.S8C56 2001   158.1
QBI01-200375

Unless otherwise noted, all quotations are from
The Book of Positive Quotations
compiled and arranged by John Cook, 1996, Fairview Press.

Contents

viii

ction   *x*

Traits   *xii*

Reinforcing Your *Belief System*

pter 1   **Be a *Fearless* Kid Again**   *2*
ith Carlos Figueroa

g a trip around the world with his bride-to-be was Carlos' dream. The
was that he had no money. Discover how he made his dream come true.

y topics: • *The 3AM meeting* • *Risk Taking* • *Visualization* • *Breakthrough*
Embracing Change
tivity: ***Breaking Patterns with the 3AM Meeting***

pter 2   **Believe in Yourself**   *10*
with Nancy Kruse

e she was five Nancy dreamed of being an animator. Growing up she loved
cartoons and practiced and practiced. While in college she wanted to be a
new animated television series. She followed her dream.

ey topics: • *Self-esteem* • *Self-knowledge* • *Visualization* • *Perseverance*
Doing what you love • *Believing you can do it*
ctivity: ***Reinforcing Self-Esteem***

apter 3   **Relaunch Yourself**   *16*
with Michael James

a comfortable job and started all over again. Little did Michael know that he
ave to give up everything to rekindle his dream.

ey topics: • *Starting over* • *Tenacity* • *Seeking a new challenging job*
Support of others • *Never give up* • *Strong faith* • *Learning new skills*
ctivity: ***Reinventing Yourself***

apter 4   **The Will to Achieve**   *22*
with Debbie Murray

velfare mother to secretary to systems integration consultant, Debbie was

To the members of

Success Builders Interna

A Personal Development Org

for their continuous encouragemer

to help me reach my goc

Also to my husband,

Don M.,

for believing in me these past

and letting me be free

to explore whatever I wanted

Prefac

Introd

Top 1(

Part

Ch

Visualiz
challeng

K
•
A

Ch

Ever si
to draw
part of

C

He qu
would

(

From

determined to get what she wanted. She saw an opportunity and latched onto it. She believed she could do anything she put her mind to.

> Key topics: • *Self-confidence. Determination* • *Practice makes perfect* • *Have a positive mental attitude* • *Stay focused*
> Activity: *Reinforcing Willpower*

Chapter 5   The Motivating Factor for Success   *30*
with Loc Van Phan

A Vietnam refugee, Loc had unbeatable determination to survive and succeed in his life. He escaped South Vietnam in 1979 by boat with 46 other desperate people. He came to America with only $50 and spoke no English. He wanted to be a part of the American Dream.

> Key topics: *Unbeatable determination* • *Never give up* • *Keep Hope Alive*
> Activity: *Dismantling Barriers*

Part II   Boosting Your *Self-Motivation*

Chapter 6   Enthusiasm: The Greatest Energy Booster   *40*
with Chao Huang

Enthusiasm is rampant in Chao's life today as he enjoys creating new ideas on the Internet. Yet there was a time when enthusiasm was absent from Chao's life. He learned that with enthusiasm he could develop new businesses, create new ideas, and others wanted to get involved in his businesses.

> Key topics: • *Being in "The Zone"* • *Excitement* • *Enthusiasm is contagious* • *Burning Desire* • *Supreme confidence* • *Do the things you passionately love*
> Activity: *Rekindling Enthusiasm*

Chapter 7   Trust Begins With You   *48*
with Dave Latner

He had a dream to travel around the world. Dave felt it was time to "recharge his batteries." He was terrified to travel around the world alone, but he did it anyway.

> Key topics: • *Trusting others* • *Learning to accept the kindness of other people* • *Practicing assertiveness* • *Taking charge of your life*
> Activity: *Balancing Your Life*

Chapter 8   Timid as a Mouse No More!   *54*
with Joan Clout-Kruse

Shyness and social anxiety prevented Joan from doing all the things she wanted to do. She was determined to change. She discovered that timidity and social anxiety are learned behaviors. She learned new ways to cope with shyness.

Key topics: • *Overcoming extreme shyness* • *Discovering the joy of boldness* • *Overcoming social anxiety* • *Pay attention to your successes, learn from your mistakes*
Activity: *Strengthening Your Boldness*

Chapter 9   Stuck? Find a Buddy and Commit!   *60*

with Marc Isaac Potter

He had a burning desire to be a seminar leader but Marc got stuck. He called a friend for support and to help him get unstuck. That experience led him to develop a program to help others work together to get what they want.

Key topics: • *Practicing commitment, self-reliance, trust, and cooperative skills* • *Working with a partner* • *Getting unstuck* • *Setting goals and doing it*
Activity: *Rekindling Commitment*

Chapter 10   Hope is the Mainspring in Life   *68*

with Kilsoon Kim *and* Jinsoo Terry

An amazing Korean woman, Kilsoon, kept on going even though there seemed to be no way out. She overcame any barrier that got in the way of achieving her dreams for her children even when she lost her husband and her house. She never gave up hope. She had a dream for her oldest daughter—to send Jinsoo to college to become an engineer.

Key topics: • *Keep hope alive* • *Never look back* • *Keep on going* • *Encouragement and support* • *Overcome your fears* • *Having faith in yourself and others*
Activity: *Keeping Hope Alive*

Part III   Building Your *New Life Plan*

Chapter 11   Build Your Network   *74*

with Cesar Plata

He had a dream to create a network for Latinos. He believed that by connecting with other people you could enhance your opportunities for personal and business growth.

Key topics: • *It's who knows you that counts* • *Spread your name around* • *Tell us about yourself* • *Networking can bring you the success you want*
Activity: *Developing Your Network of Contacts*

Chapter 12   Share Your Passion   *82*

with Gail Turner

She was the first woman to build her own aircraft and fly solo across the country. She knows that "sharing your passion" works. With perseverance and tenacity she made her dreams come true.

Key topics: • *Visualization* • *Don't let go of your dream* • *Ask for help* • *Share your passion with others* • *Perseverance and tenacity can help you achieve your goals*
Activity: *Planning the Rest of Your Life*

Contents

Preface   *viii*

Introduction   *x*

Top 10 Traits   *xii*

Part I   Reinforcing Your *Belief System*

Chapter 1   Be a *Fearless* Kid Again   *2*

with Carlos Figueroa

Visualizing a trip around the world with his bride-to-be was Carlos' dream. The challenge was that he had no money. Discover how he made his dream come true.

> **Key topics:** • *The 3AM meeting* • *Risk Taking* • *Visualization* • *Breakthrough* • *Embracing Change*
>
> **Activity:** *Breaking Patterns with the 3AM Meeting*

Chapter 2   Believe in Yourself   *10*

with Nancy Kruse

Ever since she was five Nancy dreamed of being an animator. Growing up she loved to draw cartoons and practiced and practiced. While in college she wanted to be a part of a new animated television series. She followed her dream.

> **Key topics:** • *Self-esteem* • *Self-knowledge* • *Visualization* • *Perseverance* • *Doing what you love* • *Believing you can do it*
>
> **Activity:** *Reinforcing Self-Esteem*

Chapter 3   Relaunch Yourself   *16*

with Michael James

He quit a comfortable job and started all over again. Little did Michael know that he would have to give up everything to rekindle his dream.

> **Key topics:** • *Starting over* • *Tenacity* • *Seeking a new challenging job* • *Support of others* • *Never give up* • *Strong faith* • *Learning new skills*
>
> **Activity:** *Reinventing Yourself*

Chapter 4   The Will to Achieve   *22*

with Debbie Murray

From welfare mother to secretary to systems integration consultant, Debbie was

To the members of

Success Builders International,

A Personal Development Organization,

for their continuous encouragement and support

to help me reach my goals.

Also to my husband,

Don M.,

for believing in me these past 38 years

and letting me be free

to explore whatever I wanted to be.

Chapter 13   Hold On To Your Dream   *88*

with Don "atomicboy" Kruse

He had a solid vision years ago yet the business never got off the ground. Don continued to develop his skills and knows that someday soon he will be able to rekindle his dream.

Key topics: • *Self-confidence* • *Visualization* • *Following your dream*
• *Networking* • *Breaking out of your comfort zone* • *Skills you learn will pay off in the future*
Activity: *Renewing Your Dreams*

Chapter 14   Follow Your Bliss   *94*

with Doug Jones

In 1990 he opened his business on a spiritual impulse on April Fools Day with $600. Today Doug Jones' mortgage company is a multi-million dollar business. His philosophy is to "visualize what you want and believe it will happen."

Key topics*: • Developing a clear vision • Believing in yourself • Giving back to the community • Sharing your vision with your staff • Following your spirituality • Enjoying life*
Activity: *: Goal Setting in the Park*

Chapter 15   Unleash Your Creativity   *100*

with Sal Dossani

From computer consultant to president of a travel agency and a storyteller, Sal believes in using his imagination and inspiration for his success. Never give up the quest to achieve your heart's desires.

Key topics: • *Enjoy life • Learning is a lifelong experience • Living life with complete freedom from inner desires • Educate yourself • Helping others can make your own life richer and more rewarding*
Activity: *Unleashing Creativity*

Acknowledgements   *107*

List of Contributors   *108*

Footnotes   *112*

About the Author   *113*

Order Form   *114*

I N today's world everyone must take charge of his or her career, business and personal life. We must be free agents who take responsibility for our own learning. Pensions are fading into the past, a job-for-life is no more, and Social Security alone is not enough to retire to a comfortable, independent life. All of us must become self-reliant and free agents. "Be your own rock... rule your kingdom,"[1] said business guru, Tom Peters. We must be self-determined and not wait for opportunity to come to us. "We must find ways to make our own opportunities," said Gail Turner, the dynamo gal who built two airplanes and whose story is in this book. Ralph Waldo Emerson said it so well, "Unless you try to do something beyond what you have already mastered, you will never grow."

This book invites you to take a glimpse into the hearts of some amazing people. They came from Silicon Valley in Northern California, yet they are not all geeks and techno-experts. They are entrepreneurs, Corporate America professionals and executives, volunteers, working moms/dads/singles, covering a wide range of diversity and ages from 30- to 60-something and coming from vastly different backgrounds. A few are millionaires, some are working towards it, and for all, a large bank account is not the primary motivating factor for success in their lives. They have dreams just like you.

They have faced many challenges and disappointments in their lives, yet they didn't allow anything to stop them.

In the pages to follow, you'll meet these dynamic people who took many different roads to get where they are today. They are dreamers, motivators, role models, survivors, and above all achievers. They have one thing in common: They stepped out of their comfortable world and ventured into the unknown in order to follow a dream. They had one passion: to do something they really, really wanted to do. This book invites you to hope and to believe that you too can achieve your dreams just as these very special people have done.

You will meet Kilsoon Kim, a Korean refugee who lost her parents and siblings during the separation and closing of the North and South Korea borders in the '40s. She believed passionately that education was the key to her children's success and followed that dream despite the financial challenges in her life. Doug Jones, CEO of Mortgage Magic, prioritizes having fun on the job. "If the company folded tomorrow, I would still know that everyone had fun," he says. Michael James's goal was to start all over in his career. Little did he know that he would have to give up everything to achieve his dream. You'll meet Carlos Figueroa, who visualized traveling around the world with his bride-to-be although he had no money at the time. You will read the incredible story of Loc Van Phan who escaped from Vietnam by boat. He took a 2000-mile ocean journey with the hope of freedom and security.

In order to reinforce and enhance your road to success, there are stories on managing shyness, supercharging your commitment attitude, rekindling enthusiasm, and working with a buddy to help you get what you want.

Amazing stories? Yes. This book is living proof that the impossible happens to ordinary people every day. Yet this is not a book of fiction. These are real people living in the real world. They succeeded in doing what they wanted to do by believing in themselves, working hard, staying with their idea, getting help from others, mustering talents they never knew they had, making personal sacrifices, and conjuring a faith and passion so powerful that they overcame any obstacle that got in their way.

Introducing
Silicon Valley Dynamos
and How to Use This Book

MANY of my friends, colleagues, acquaintances and even my children are part of Silicon Valley—and not all of them are Silicon Valley geeks but rather Silicon Valley dynamos. This definitely is a new dynamic world today. The people in this book are part of the new high-tech world even though many of them are not working directly in that environment. They have lived and worked in the Silicon Valley area in Northern California and they have moved and changed as needed to succeed in this world.

Born in San Francisco, I have seen the birth, changes and growth of Silicon Valley over the years—from fruit orchards to campus-type buildings. Silicon Valley has no borders. It is not a city or a county. Its geographical area is defined by the imagination of the people who live and work in these high-tech areas. Other communities are now claiming they too have a Silicon Valley in their cities and in other countries. It is a place where today the Internet and high-tech companies reside to the point that they create thousands of jobs and opportunities—along with traffic jams, expensive homes, geeks, stock options, millionaires and wannabe millionaires.

These success stories are here to encourage you to persevere and stay with your dreams. They might give you the nudge you need to take stronger action towards your goals and practice new techniques to break old habits. Thus, this book, *Top 10 Traits of Silicon Valley Dynamos*, was born.

Bite Size Lessons

Designed for the busy person, the chapters are short. You can read one chapter on your lunch hour. Learning is a lifelong experience. Each chapter has an activity that gives you tips and exercises that you can practice to help you break patterns and reinforce your new belief system. We learn by doing, so if you want to reinforce some area of your behavioral life, practice the activities. You can start anywhere you want in this book. Pick a chapter that interests you.

These activities do work. Adapt them to fit your needs. Some of the activities may appear in more than one chapter with a different slant, as repetition is an effective process for learning powerful new good habits. With practice and repetition you can learn new ways to achieve your goals and make positive changes in your life. It depends on your willingness to change to get what you want. Enjoy some great adventures as you read about the experiences of these amazing Silicon Valley dynamos.

Joan Clout-Kruse
Foster City, California

Top 10 Traits of Silicon Valley Dynamos

ALL of the Silicon Valley dynamos who you will meet in this book look at life with a positive frame of mind; they are full of faith, hope and dreams. No doubt about it: Successful people are dreamers, movers and shakers. While others talk about their aspirations, achievers actualize theirs. They don't wait for the right time, right weather or approval from others—they jump in and take charge. And, they definitely have a lot of fun along the way as they explore, discover, plan and act on their visions.

You will notice the 10 traits listed below appearing repeatedly in the stories that follow.

1. Believe in Yourself.

Be positive. Be bold. The role models in this book are assertive and confident in their decisions and activities—they believe they can do what they aim to do. And they know that the only limits that really count are the ones people place upon themselves. Looking for the good in other people, dynamos approach life with enthusiasm.

2. Educate Yourself.

Knowledge is power—increased knowledge strengthens self-esteem. The dynamic people presented here practice honing their skills every day; learning is a lifelong habit they enjoy. They operate like Olympians who practice their skills daily for success—they read, attend seminars, take higher-learning classes, find mentors, and learn everything they can on the job. To get what they want, they're willing to go the extra mile in search of answers. With childlike ingenuousness, they're willing to ask questions of knowledgeable people who have the answers they need to reach success. Their self-knowledge and learning have given them skills enabling them to become an accomplished artist, magician, animator, Internet expert, seminar leader, Web designer, financial leader, television news photographer, real estate investor, engineer, systems integration expert, and computer operating systems technical expert. And, besides all that, their collective repertoire includes building airplanes, starting a business, buying and learning a new business, writing and publishing a book, and creating a nonprofit organization. Most of these skills were self-taught (with the exception of those that required a higher-learning degree, such as becoming an engineer, teacher, etc).

3. *Work with Winners.*

Super achievers know enough to ask for help and advice. No one succeeds alone. When making an uncomfortable change is necessary, they garner support. Marc Isaac Potter "got stuck" writing a manual and asked a friend to help. Cesar Plata's whole concept of developing a virtual and real network of Latino professionals was based on the concept that connecting with each other is important for success. Gail Turner had thirty friends help her build her second airplane; they came because her dream and her enthusiasm inspired them, and most important, she asked.

4. *Take Risks.*

Dynamos push through their fear. They persevere and see failure in perspective, rather than experiencing an obstacle as the ending. They try other routes until they find one that works. Seeing risks as challenges and opportunities, they push through fear by taking more risks. Michael James quit a comfortable job to learn a new career—even when he lost all his material possessions and had very little money, he never gave up. Loc Van Phan literally risked his life to escape Vietnam.

5. *Exercise the Will to Change.*

Motivators' inner strength keeps them on course. "Will is like a muscle–it grows stronger when you exercise it regularly," said change expert, Dr. Sidney B. Simon[2]. Silicon Valley Dynamos produce enough will to stay with any course of action they choose. Debbie Murray went ahead with a typing test required for a better job although her fingers were in pain from a window slamming down on them the night before. Dave Latner left his comfortable environment to travel around the world although initially he was fearful about embarking on the journey. Dynamos are passionate about their dreams—and they approach their goals creatively, open-mindedly, embracing change, and frequently looking for new opportunities.

6. Cultivate Faith and Spirituality.

Many dynamic people find that their faith in God helps them   navigate the steps necessary to reach their goals. Doug Jones initiated his company on a spiritual impulse. Michael James gave up his occupation and embarked on a new career living with the promise; "I can do all things through Christ who strengthens me." Marc Isaac Potter meditates daily. And, Joan Clout-Kruse prays for guidance and direction in her daily life. Believing in a higher power keeps hope alive—for many, prayer and/or meditation are a daily practice that helps strengthen their faith and keep them on course.

7. Keep Hope Alive.

Visionaries always see alternatives to problems, light at the end of the tunnel. They look for options and ways to achieve their goals. Kilsoon Kim maintained hope that her children would be well educated—even after she lost her husband and her home. Don Kruse continues to believe that he will rekindle his dream of opening a digital photo printing store.

8. Visualize and Dream.

Dynamos clearly imagine reaching their goal. They see the end result in their mind's eye and then turn their dreams into reality. They know what it takes to achieve their dreams, and they persevere until they reach their goal. Marc Isaac Potter dreamed about being a seminar leader and passionately pursued that goal. Gail Turner dreamed about building an airplane although she didn't know how to do it; she envisioned and believed it would happen. In his business Mortgage Magic, Doug Jones practices visualization and goal setting with his staff during planning meetings.

9. *Embrace Excellence.*

Achievers compete with themselves and attain excellence by challenging themselves to do better. Most avoid those deadly energy drainers: procrastination and perfectionism. Successful people practice self-improvement each day. Even if what they do isn't perfect, they remain flexible and keep on going. Carlos Figueroa challenges himself to try new things every day. And, at the same time, when he says yes, he keeps his promises. Chao Huang, Internet guru, has developed several Internet businesses and tests himself daily against his high standard of quality, stretching himself to stay informed of the rapid changes in this field.

10. *Give Back to the Community.*

Dynamos' talent and energy overflow to help other people and the community. As mentors and role models, they donate their time to train and teach others. Sal Dossani, president of a travel agency, is working with a new form of communication training to help others succeed with their ambitions. Marc Isaac Potter volunteers his time to help children improve their self-esteem. Doug Jones contributes to the community by performing volunteer magic shows for children's organizations as well as serving on the board of the Salvation Army. Cesar Plata, through the network he developed, has helped countless people find jobs, build their businesses and meet a myriad of other needs—most at no cost to the individuals using his services. Each person presented in this book has helped others and felt rewarded in the experience.

Part I
Reinforcing Your
Belief System

SELF-ESTEEM is fleeting. It needs frequent strengthening, support and reinforcement. Before most of our goals in life can be accomplished, we must believe in ourselves. Self-defeat, negativity, fear, despair, ambivalence, perceived inadequacies and other barriers might prevent us from being all that we want to be.

To build self-esteem, we need to receive moral support from our positive-thinking friends, continuously take small risks, increase our self-knowledge, and exercise our assertiveness. We affirm ourselves by saying yes more often to life challenges and possibilities and saying no more often to self-defeating pursuits and activities that don't attract us. We increase our self-confidence when we set a goal, make a plan, and stick to it.

In the following chapters, you will meet some unique people whose lives express self-determination, perseverance and self-confidence. They believe in themselves. Their stories are living proof that we can do anything we want to do with determination and belief in ourselves. Positive self-esteem promotes success.

Chapter 1

Be a *Fearless* Kid Again

"There are no risks, only adventures."

—

Carlos Figueroa

with Carlos Figueroa

THREE o'clock in the wee hours of the morning, and there I was interviewing my good friend Carlos Figueroa in a booth at Denny's Restaurant in San Jose (the southern end of Silicon Valley). The peculiar meeting time had a reason—such a good reason, in fact, that it has become a key training tool and a tradition for us to meet at this hour.

Carlos broached the idea of "The 3:00 A.M. Meeting" a few of years ago while working on a new action plan as part of a committee. "Let's meet at 3:00 A.M. to discuss our long-range plans," he said to the group. A moment of silence fell upon the eighteen members attending the meeting. They just looked at each other, perplexed.

"What?!" Some echoed.

Carlos smiled and dared the others with a rhetorical, "Sure why not? It is a great way to get out of your comfort zone and reach a higher level of emotional well-being by meeting a challenge you set for yourself. I promise, you will get more done than you would otherwise." Reluctantly, everyone mumbled in agreement that they would meet at 3:00 A.M.

That Saturday morning, ten brave souls showed up to meet at Denny's for what proved to be a pivotal and fun meeting. They accomplished the goals for their meeting as stated on the agenda. And, over time they recognized that they shared a valuable bond with each other—together they had experienced the meaningful event of breaking one of their typical patterns in that early morning hour.

If anything could be described as routine in Carlos's life, it would be his habit of challenging himself daily to break his patterns and to be primed for the opportunity to change. He plans to live the rest of his life daring to be different from the norm. His favorite saying is, "It shall be done!" He is a courageous kid.

✳   ✳   ✳

WHEN I was fourteen, I discovered the value of getting up at 2:00 or 3:00 AM to do something I really wanted to do when no one else was around to bother me. I began by sneaking outside the house to try out the family car while everyone was asleep. In short time, I learned how to drive the car and was navigating it around the block, and later, down the streets of San Francisco. My mother (who raised me on her own) knew nothing about these escapades.

Unencumbered, I extended my jaunts to restaurants and other places where I could meet people. Off I went following my curiosity to explore San Francisco's neighborhoods. Good things happen at that hour—the mind is not disturbed at 3:00 A.M.

Soon, leaving the house in the early morning hours became self-discipline for me. I saw it as an opportunity at hand to break barriers and make new discoveries. There are no risks, only adventures. Each experience raises a person's consciousness. I always want to move to the next level in my life experiences.

Do you remember some of your adventures as a child? You probably had no fear, or very little fear, when you tried something new. Each day, I looked forward to the opportunity to break more patterns of my daily life. I was an inquisitive child and relished new experiences.

My boyish adventures included a thrilling jump off a high beam at Sutro Baths in San Francisco, a beam several peoples' height above the waters. One day in my youth, I jumped into murky waters to save a boy from drowning—bystanders looked on, too fearful to act. Daring as that might seem to some, I believe a person can do anything they want if their feelings are unfettered by doubt.

That year, I happened to find two books on a streetcar seat that ended up opening new gateways to my personal growth. One was a psychological study by Sigmund Freud, which lead me to explore the way the mind works. The other book discussed the wealthiest men in the world, revealing that they were all in real estate. Continuing to trust the path directed by my curiosity, I ventured to the library to learn all I could about real estate.

I took my next step with self-confidence: I acquired my first property while still underage. After negotiating with the agent to buy the property, I persuaded my mother to sign the papers. Then, I followed up with studying all I could about investing in property.

Visualizing what you want has a tremendous power on the mind. When I was twenty-six, I wanted to ask the girl of my dreams, Ileana, for her hand in marriage. I had been seeing her for four years, yet I didn't have the nerve to ask her.

Then one day Ileana and I were browsing through a travel magazine. "How would you like to go to Japan on our honeymoon?" I asked impulsively and excitedly, showing her the beautiful photograph of Japan in the magazine.

"Okay," Ileana said, sounding quite happy.

I was so excited. I understood that between the lines Ileana had said that she would marry me. I was too elated to sleep that night. Although I had no money for the trip I'd offered, first thing the next morning I visited a travel agent to find out what such a trip would cost.

The travel agent caught my excitement and expanded it, "You should travel around the world," she proposed. She walked me to a globe and pointed out all the places she suggested I tour, having me visualize what it was going to be like to travel all over the world.

The next day, I showed Ileana all the brochures. She too reverberated with the excitement. I was exhilarated by her affirmations and belief in me, but then when I was driving home, reality sunk in. I pondered, *How is this going to happen?*

I couldn't sleep the next morning. Aimlessly driving around San Francisco in the early hours, I thought about how to make this trip a reality—after all, Ileana believed in me and said she would marry me. I continued to visualize the various countries the travel agent had shown me on the globe and in the brochures: Denmark, Switzerland, Japan, Italy, and more. I seriously wanted this trip to happen.

With no notion of how to pay for the honeymoon, I kept driving and driving, struggling with my thoughts, *God help me. How am I going to finance this?*

A few moments later, I noticed a woman who was washing her stairs; she was surrounded by a group of purring cats.

Stirred by an impulse to stop and talk to her, I parked my car, stepped out and greeted her with, "Hello, let me help you," Within no time, I began helping her clean her sidewalk—garbed in my spiffy new dark business suit. When we had finished, she invited me to join her for a snack in the house, where I met a myriad of more friendly, purring cats. The lady began bathing the felines, who were obviously enjoying this ritual, as she spoke to me.

"What are you doing out here?" she asked.

An idea sparked off in my mind. I replied, "I'm looking for a house to buy," mustering a serious, businesslike look on my face.

"Really?" she responded. "I've got a nutty friend who is going to sell her house. She believes God is going to send her a buyer."

I recognized that moment of opportunity, or perhaps destiny, and later went to the friend's house. I knocked on the door, introduced myself, and said, "I want to buy a house." Overjoyed, the woman was positive that God had sent me.

My plea to God while driving was answered as well. I made a deal and bought her house with no money down.

With gusto, I began fixing up the house with the intention that this would become Ileana's and my home. Before I could complete the renovation, however, a friend of the family saw it and wanted to buy it. So, I turned it around for a profit—in cash.

The house sale proved to be a watershed event for me, the first of many house sales I completed. Everywhere I went I would stop and talk to people in stores and on the street. "I'm looking for a house to buy," I would say, which would generate more leads and opportunities to buy houses, fix and sell them.

Within three months I had accumulated enough money for my fantasized trip around the world. Ileana and I married and I became a successful real estate investor—self-taught.

I have no fear in trying anything new. Risks are new adventures that I look forward to doing. Most people are conditioned to avoid going beyond what they know. We have to let the little child in us continue to flicker. With the innocence of the child within us we can do anything.

My mother gave me all the encouragement I needed as a child. She told me many times, "Whatever your mind can envision, just believe, believe, believe that you can do it."

My mother was right. Dream and visualize what you want in life. Know that the world is full of possibilities. Believe in yourself and anything is possible. Be different and be a fearless kid again. Discover new things and enjoy your adventure along the way.

Breaking Patterns with the 3:00 A.M. Meeting

☐ Go ahead and plan a 3:00 A.M. meeting with some friends and colleagues. You will break self-imposed patterns with very little risk. Your benefits are many:

1. Actualize more of your potential to meet your goals and be account able to yourself: Yes, you can get up at 2:00 A.M. to get to a 3:00 A.M. meeting.

2. Determine your actions from your beliefs despite any fear of ridicule from others; break the mold.

3. Eliminate self-imposed constraints; break old habits.

4. Take charge of your life.

5. Enjoy a sense of accomplishment—like being on a launch pad and blasting off.

☐ Invite like-minded people to come to your 3:00 A.M. meeting. Have a purpose. Consider these possibilities:

1. Plan an event together.

2. Share goals with each other and each commit to take their particular first step.

3. Brainstorm some common challenge or new idea.

4. Decide on vacation plans together.

5. Discuss parenting tips.

6. Develop a self-help group.

7. Create an action plan for your life.

8. Come up with your own topic or idea.

☐ At the end of the meeting, discuss how each of you felt before, during and after it. I believe you will want to do it again and again.

Chapter 2
Believe
in Yourself

Nancy Kruse, Age 10

"*Nobody is ever born a great anything.*
People learn and develop."

—

Holly Stiel[3]

with Nancy Kruse

SELF-ESTEEM is built on a foundation of feeling good about yourself and about how others feel towards you. Do you like who you are? Do you believe you are competent enough to achieve your dreams? Those questions are important—though rather blunt and direct. Your answers will shape your belief system. People who believe in themselves are more motivated, positive and open to change. The more you like yourself, the less likely you are to hurt yourself emotionally,

Nancy Kruse learned definitively when she was eight years old that practice builds self-confidence. With revelation, she recognized that she must do the things she loved to be happy. She had neither doubt nor fear. She knew what she wanted and went after it with a fierce conviction of her ability to do it. To achieve all that we want out of life, we must believe in ourselves just like Nancy did.

✳   ✳   ✳

WHEN I was eight years old I loved art and also drawing cartoons. Every moment that I could, I drew something. I aspired to grow up to be like Charles Schulz—drawing characters like Snoopy and Charlie Brown.

One day, right after we moved to a new neighborhood, I felt terribly lonely. I went to my mother and told her—tears streaming down my face—that I was lonely and had no one to play with. I asked her to stay home instead of going to work so she could play with me.

My mother paused briefly to reflect on my words, and then she picked up some of my drawings off a nearby table and said, "Nancy, you love to draw, don't you?"

I wiped my eyes and said, "Yes."

"What would happen if I took away your crayons and said you couldn't draw anymore?"

I was taken aback. Searching her eyes to see whether she was serious, I replied, "Mommy, you wouldn't do that, would you? I have to draw!"

"No, I wouldn't, Honey. But that is the same way I would feel if I had to quit my job. I love it. If I had to quit, I would be terribly sad."

After a brief moment of thought I said, "Okay," attempting to understand the situation. "I don't want you to quit your job if you love it." Even though I was only eight, I saw it was important to do what you love. I didn't want my mother to be sorrowful from quitting work.

So I continued drawing cartoons, and I taught myself advanced drawing through library books. Anytime I wanted to learn something new, I perused material at the library. In addition, I learned origami and juggling. Soon I realized that the library was full of "how to" books and I could learn almost anything there. I increased my confidence level by continuing to learn new things—mostly in the creative, artistic field because that was my passion. As time passed, I felt that I could learn to do anything and draw anything I pleased.

Until I was in junior high school, I wanted to be an animator at Disney Studios; I was disappointed by their films in the late '70s, however, and decided to become a fine artist instead. I took several art classes in junior high school. My voracious love for art showed in everything I did: Drawing was an obsession with me—I couldn't help myself. I scribbled a cartoon here and there on almost every piece of paper I touched. Every margin in a book, or blank page I saw, "cried out to me" to be embellished with some artwork.

I hadn't planned on going to college, but then one of my high school teachers told me about "art college." After investigating the possibilities, one day I came home and matter of factly announced to my mother, "I'm going to go to Otis Parsons Art Institute when I graduate."

"Otis, who?" she said, completely ignorant of art colleges.

Proudly and firmly I said, "Otis Parsons in Los Angeles. My art teacher suggested I apply. I'm going to be a fine artist."

"An art degree," she said. "Don't you want to go to a business college?"

"Business college? Are you nuts?! No!" I asserted. "Otis is my first choice, but I'll apply to others. And I'll go on to get a masters degree so I can teach fine art." I had no idea how fine artists made a living but I figured as a last resort I could become an art teacher.

In 1983 I did go to Otis. I studied every type of art form. I'd proudly present my parents with six-foot by eight-foot wall murals on canvas, soldered metal objects, and uniquely designed wooden boxes that were hammered together with carpenter's nails and enthusiasm. Mom and dad graciously accepted these huge pieces of art that I brought home. In my junior year I decided that animation remained my true interest. More and more of the projects I worked on were films, and I decided to continue my education at UCLA, working on a master's degree in animation.

In 1988, the full-length animated movie *Roger Rabbit* came out; in short time, the demand for animation artists accelerated as other studios began producing animated movies. Then in 1989, I heard about a new animated television series that was planned for production. No successful adult animated television show had come out since *The Flintstones*. I yearned to be a part of this new series.

I requested the opportunity to show my student film and sketchbook to the producer, and she told me that I'd be a great animator "someday." I left there feeling great until I realized that "someday" meant not now.

The next two weeks I called the producer almost daily to see when I could join this animation venture. Finally, my persistence paid off: I was hired as a background clean-up artist. Although I had no idea what that was, I trusted that I could figure it out.

Today, *The Simpsons* is the longest-running sitcom on television. It is in its 12th season and still going strong. After holding almost every type of production job on the series, I currently serve as one of the directors. The show has won many Emmys and Annie awards (animation awards) including "The Best Animated Show in a Prime-Time Television Series."

I believe that it is better to try and fail than to never try anything at all. I knew that I could learn anything that I didn't know. Whatever we want in life is ours for the asking. To learn and grow along the way, we just have to believe that we can do it.

Reinforcing Self-Esteem

Be your own best friend—focus on the positive things that happen in your life and let go of the negative. To help build self-confidence, try some of these activities:

☐ *Take intellectual risks.* Identify activities you can do to strengthen your belief system and then do one of them. Perhaps it's reading an inspirational or motivational book; or, maybe it's going back to school, learning something new from a library book, or taking some workshops. You could learn to play a musical instrument, take singing lessons or join a choir.

☐ *Evaluate your day.* Develop the habit of taking a quick ten-minute inventory of your day before you go to bed. Recount all the good things that you accomplished. Fast forward past any negative things that happened— they are over and it's time to think of the positive events of your day. Stay focused on the positive parts of your daily life.

☐ *Save positive notes and records.* Keep a file of affirmative letters and e-mails that you receive. Into the file throw meaningful positive quotations you heard during the day and anything else that helped you feel great. Review this file at least once a month—more often when needed to maintain your confidence and positive attitude.

☐ *Take emotional risks.* Meet new people, and go new places. Return a smile and say, "Hi." Assert yourself by saying, "No," when that's what you really want to say.

☐ *Take physical risks.* Take up in-line skating. Or, perhaps you want to ride a motorcycle, run in a race or climb a mountain. Try something new that involves a little risk. Push yourself to do something you haven't done before, but be intelligent and sensible about it.

Chapter 3
Relaunch
Yourself

*"Without faith, a man can do nothing;
with it, all things are possible."*

—

William Osler

with Michael James

IN 1991, Michael James joined the Foster City Toastmasters Club. This twenty-something African American was enthusiastic and eager to improve his speaking skills and anxious to learn from others in the club. He accomplished all that plus more. In fact, he strengthened his self-confidence to the point that one day he decided to quit his comfortable, well-paying job to rekindle his true aspiration.

✳   ✳   ✳

ONE afternoon in 1992, my brother and I stood in front of Mann's Chinese Theater studying the stars names on the Walk of Fame. A CBS television representative who was doing a survey on a television show approached me. At that moment, I suddenly recalled the excitement and fun I had had ten years before while working as part of a television production class at a local college. The excitement and challenge were tremendous—learning how to be a TV camera operator, editor, and director, and getting to participate in every aspect of creating a TV show.

As I stood outside of Mann's Chinese Theater, I realized with conviction that I wanted to work in the TV business. Even if I would have to give up everything to do it, I would. Little did I know at the time the challenge those very words would prophesy.

I was miserable on my job at the time; it no longer stimulated me. So, within two months after my encounter with the CBS TV representative, I quit my job and began working on reaching my dream job even though I had no money to fall back on.

First, I found the Broadcast Skills Bank in San Francisco: This nonprofit group helped me decide how to do what I wanted to do. They gave me leads for potential jobs and helped me prepare a résumé. To supplement my income, I took any kind of temporary job I could—I worked as a receptionist, did surveys, data entry, and—until my own car was repossessed— delivered pizza.

It got bad. I wondered whether I could continue to live like this. With very little money and no car, it was difficult to get around. Then, I found a job as a volunteer with KCRT, a cable access station in Richmond, California. This was great experience for me. I learned to edit, and I also learned how to do camera work, graphics, and audio and field interviews. I interviewed the mayor, the police chief and other dignitaries. And, although they didn't pay me, everyone was fed; so I worked for food, which was great for me at the time.

1994 was a crucial year. The economy was bad, and I needed money and more experience. In California, television jobs were very competitive—it was hard to break in. I decided that I needed to go to a smaller market. My brother Gary, who was in the television industry in Rochester, New York, told me about a television job in Augusta, Georgia. I was lucky to have my father, who lived in Augusta, encourage me to come and live with him until I found a job. Soon after, I decided to leave for Augusta to follow my dream.

CBS affiliate WRDW in Augusta hired me on to work, part-time at first, as a video editor for the newscast. Exciting! This was my first real job in television. I felt as though a monkey had just jumped off my back, giving me relief and peace for the first time in a year. The tremendous weight I had carried for more than a year had been lifted. I worked there for two years, which I enjoyed.

In 1996, contacts I had made in the industry led me to an opportunity to move to New York State and work for a small station in Elmira as a news videographer. I took the chance and gained even more experience.

Five months later, my brother Gary again told me about a job; this one was with NBC affiliate WSTM-TV in Syracuse. I was interviewed by then–chief photographer Frank Rossi, who hired me on the spot. (We all called Frank "Chief.") WSTM-TV is my home now; the people I work with are supportive and we work together like a family. We work hard—and I love it. I have something very special here working as a news photographer: I cover murders, fires, accidents and anything else that makes news. Sometimes we must trudge through a foot and a half of snow to get to the story. I love my work and I know that the job I do influences people's lives.

My success didn't stop there, though. Now I had time to focus on other areas of my life, and I decided it was time to meet a woman I could have a strong relationship with. I dialed up the Internet and logged onto **www.match.com**. The first week, three women responded to my profile. I began to correspond with a woman who lived just two hours away from me and with whom I shared many interests. A month or so later, she came to Syracuse to meet me. We dated for several more months—then, in December of 1998, we married.

Success doesn't happen overnight. In my case I had to let go of all the security I had with the hope that I would reach my vision. As you can tell by my story, I am joyful and satisfied with my new life. Meeting my wife was a miracle greater than I expected. Here are some tips that can help you get what you want:

1. **Never give up; keep focused on your goal.**

2. **Surround yourself with many supportive people.**

3. **If you want to get into broadcasting, focus very intently on what you want to do: Focus on radio, TV or the Internet. Although you may have to go to cities you don't initially like, do it anyway to acquire the experience. And, remember to have fun.**

There were times that I endured a lot of pain, anxiety and doubt, but my faith in God kept me going. I lived and breathed the Bible verse, Phil. 4:13, which says, "I can do all things through Christ that strengthens me." When people around me were negative, I would repeat this verse silently to myself, over and over again.

Supportive people had a major influence on me. My Toastmasters Club was my number one motivator through the positive, motivating feedback I received from the members. Today I am at peace—I came out of a dark tunnel and can now see the light.

Following your dreams probably won't always be easy. Many people quit because they would rather stay in mediocrity than go through the pain of change. I encourage you to follow your instincts and persevere. Life is too short to live a life of mediocrity.

Reinventing Yourself

1. List a number of ways you can learn one or more new skills to help you reach your goal. Prioritize your list. Then take that first step; tackle the first thing on your list.

_____

_____

_____

_____

_____

_____

2. List the resources that are available to support you in reaching your goal: Web sites, reference books, nonprofit organizations, government agencies, churches, role models, mentors and what ever else comes to your mind.

_____

_____

_____

_____

_____

_____

Chapter 4
The Will to Achieve

"Where there's a will, there's a way."
—
English Proverb

with Debbie Murray

ACHIEVERS *make up only five percent of the world, and non-achievers account for the other ninety-five percent,"said sales trainer Tom Hopkins.*[4] *The will to achieve cannot be imposed on you from the outside—it is a drive that must come from within; you must always aim to be a part of that five percent.*

Striving to reach a goal is easy for some, difficult for others, and impossible for many. What makes the difference in the character of a person who has the will to persist no matter what? What is it inside of them that gives them the tenacity to pursue their goal? Obstacles may slow them down, but they continue: They keep on going and going and going because they have a belief system that they can do what they aim to do, no matter what.

Through a tough time in her life, Debbie Murray had faith in herself that she could successfully "wallow through the mud" to get to the other side.

✽　　✽　　✽

TWENTY years ago, as a young mother, I was struggling. In an effort to improve my situation, I voluntarily stopped being on welfare and found work. I was trying to make ends meet—with two toddlers and an unemployed husband it was a difficult challenge; yet, I knew I had to keep on going even when the odds against me seemed insurmountable.

I worked as a purchasing clerk at Varian Associates in the early '80s. I was excited because this was my first real job. It provided benefits and a way to help care for my family.

At the time I joined Varian, all computers were controlled in a centralized area—no one had their own PC. A few years later, I heard that a secretarial position opened up in the engineering department and that they had acquired a new Apple® IIE computer. I was determined to get that job. I intuitively foresaw that knowing how to use a computer was the wave of the future. To be considered for the secretarial position, I had to take a typing test and pass at 55 words per minute (wpm). There was just one problem: I only typed 25 wpm. I had one week before the test to accelerate my typing speed!

Every night after work I went to my mother's house to practice on her IBM Selectric typewriter while she tested my speed. For more than an hour, it went from 25 to 30 to 40 to 45 wpm, and then at the end of the week it stopped at 50 wpm. I was disappointed that I hadn't reached 55 wpm, but I knew I had to proceed anyway with my current speed. After all, I thought, I had nothing to lose.

The eve of the typing test disaster struck. Battling to close a window at home, I pulled and pulled but the window wouldn't shut. Finally, I gave it one last strong tug and down it came, slamming shut on my fingers—which caused me immediate and severe pain. Quickly, I put ice on my throbbing fingers, but I could barely move them.

The next day, I went to work to take my typing test—my fingers were still throbbing. I concentrated on one goal: "Pass this typing test no matter what." And, I blocked out all thoughts of pain as I focused on typing. To my relief, I passed the test at exactly 55 wpm and got the job!

I knew then that I could do anything I wanted as long as I had the will and the passion. My mind had simply taken over during that typing test—everything was blocked out except for the one task to be accomplished. I was in "The Zone."[5]

Other opportunities with computers beckoned to me as time went on. I was one of the first in the company to learn the DEC VAX Information System. Later, I began producing graphics for the department. Eventually, I taught engineers and executives the new LAN network system at Varian and also developed the first manual to instruct others on how to troubleshoot the LAN system as well as the big console printer.

I learned as I went along. Today, more than twenty years later, I continue to learn and grow. I haven't always had this strong confidence in myself—self-confidence comes and goes in most of us in varying degrees. Having friends, colleagues and family who believed in me and gave me moral support also helped me develop my self-esteem.

My recent success as a system integration consultant included the creation and management of a distributed integration team to serve a customer consisting of forty-eight sites, located in ten regional business units. This opportunity showed me that I will continue to learn along the way and that I can do anything I put my mind to.

When I made a mistake or took a wrong turn along the way, I would try another way and eventually reached my goal. As much as possible, I avoided negative people who zap my energy.

Currently I work with a startup corporation. When my mother asked me what the product is, I said, "Well, if I tell you then I would have to shoot you!" She "got it" right away that startup people are quite serious about their business; she decided she would willingly wait for the appropriate time to hear the answer.

Activity

Reinforcing Your Willpower

How is your willpower? Can you stay focused, like Debbie did, so you will reach your goal? Or, do you get stuck and stop midstream? You can improve your will through practice; it does not just happen by thinking about it—you have to practice it.

Do you recall a time when you were doing something new and challenging in your life? You may have reached a certain point and then stopped because it was too painful or uncomfortable to continue. Otherwise, you persevered despite the anxiety feeling. Using our will means we may have to go through an unpleasant, uncomfortable emotional feeling as we break through a pattern in our life.

Try some of the exercises below to help strengthen your will. You are likely to feel uncomfortable as opposing forces in your mind battle over your choices of actions. Practice until you make the choice that is right for you and feel the joy and exhilaration from knowing that you did it. Then you can feel the satisfaction of having broken through a barrier.

Test your willpower:

☐ At work, the next time a coworker brings in sweets to share, avoid eating any. Pass by the food area a few times each day and look at the food, but refrain from eating any.

☐ Spend an evening at home, and don't turn on the television. If you succeed, try it for a second day, and then continue for the rest of the week if you can. Notice your feelings during this time.

☐ At your next social event, do something you usually don't like to do. Here are some possibilities:

1. If you drink alcohol beverages, don't drink any this time.

2. If you usually gorge yourself with food, cut back to just a few morsels and make them last the night.

3. If you have difficulty meeting and talking to strangers, exert yourself to meet five new people at this social gathering.

☐ Break patterns. Every morning and evening practice changing your usual patterns of behavior:

1. If you use your right hand to manipulate your computer mouse, learn how to use the left hand.

2. Women, change the sequence in which you put on your makeup in the morning.

3. Men, change the order in which you shave your face in the morning.

4. Get up fifteen minutes earlier than your norm to do something productive.

5. If you want to lose weight, leave some food on your plate at each meal—don't eat it all.

☐ Develop your own willpower exercises. Use activities or behaviors that you know you should change but in the past haven't had the willpower to tackle. Practice the exercises until they are no longer emotionally painful to do.

Evaluate the results:

1. After you finish some of your willpower exercises assess how you felt *before* you tested your will.

2. How did you feel *after* you tested your will?

3. How did you feel during the exercise?

4. What part was most difficult for you?

5. What did you do to overcome any negative self-talk or feelings you may have had?

6. What will you do in the future to make it easier to use your will?

Chapter 5
The Motivating
Factor for *Success*

*"Strength does not come from physical capacity.
It comes from an indomitable will."*
—

Mahatma Gandhi

with Loc Van Phan

LOC Van Phan, a refugee from Vietnam, had unbeatable determination to survive and succeed in his life. Together with forty-six other desperate people, he escaped South Vietnam in 1979 by boat. During a Dale Carnegie Training program, Loc shared his Vietnam escape story with the class participants—everyone was spellbound. His amazing story began in 1975 when he was in his last year of high school.

✳   ✳   ✳

I knew something was wrong. The U.S. soldiers had left South Vietnam, and everyone had a bad feeling that something was going to happen. Then it happened: Tanks swept through the capital city—with one fell swoop they killed almost every South Vietnamese soldier they saw. The government surrendered and the Communists took over South Vietnam. My friends and I witnessed the killing of many young soldiers; the streets were strewn with dead bodies. Students didn't know if they would be killed or spared.

When the Communists gained power, South Vietnamese currency was stripped of its value. In order to eat, we had to learn Marxist theory so that we could get our coupons stamped, which in turn allowed us to buy food. Each week we went to Marxist school and had our coupons stamped. Practically everyone was poor and had little hope that the quality of life would improve. The Communist party motivated people to join by the promise of more food and preferential treatment at the hospital.

Three years later in 1978, many young Vietnamese were being sent to Cambodia for an upcoming battle. I began attending the local Phu-Tho University to avoid joining the army and being drafted and sent into the fray. The times were rife with uncertainty and distrust; I couldn't even trust my friends for fear that they might be Communist spies.

One day I knew I had to change my life. I could no longer stand it. I saw no future for myself: If you didn't join the Communist Party, you had no future. War was about to start with Cambodia, and many would die, I was sure. I had no hope.

I thought about fleeing Vietnam, but the danger was great. If I were caught I would be sent to a "Re-Education Camp" in the jungle to restudy Marxist theory and endure hard labor for many years. We heard that the majority sent to the camps died from the hard labor and lack of food and medicine.

Finally, I decided to try escaping because I had no hope anyway if I stayed in Vietnam. So, when I was twenty years old I planned to escape by sea. The boat passage cost three ounces of gold. As I had neither gold nor money, I became a recruiter. Secretly, I recruited ten people, which earned me free passage.

This was a real-life espionage adventure: I would investigate people beforehand, following them for days to see where they went, to make sure they were not Communist spies. If I were caught, I would be put in jail for life.

We were four recruiters selecting ten people. After one year of planning and recruiting, we were ready to go. But then, just before the fishing boat was going to leave, we heard that one of the passengers was a Communist spy. All forty-four people fled from the boat before the Communists got there. The Communists took the boat, and all the money the passengers had paid was gone. I had to start over.

A year later, we made a second attempt to escape. Again, the Communists heard of the escape and everyone had to quit the plan and flee.

When I was twenty-three years old, I was on my third try. Forty-six others and I began yet again to plan our escape by boat. We used a wood fishing boat that was somewhere between fifteen and twenty feet long with neither oars nor sailing equipment. A small motor at the back was secretly replaced with a stronger, faster dual motor.

This arrangement required detailed, strategic planning—it covered a 2,200-mile trip to our destination, Hong Kong. We needed a network of people to buy a boat and fuel, food, guns and ammunition, and also to study the weather. Again, at the last minute we heard the Communists were coming.

We had to decide right away whether to go or once again abandon our plans.

This time we decided to go—even though we did not have enough food or fuel. We knew that 80 to 90 percent of those trying to escape Vietnam by boat do not get through. Against all odds, we chose to go anyway; we were determined to get through. Forty-seven people jam-packed together, we left with our leader, a former captain of the South Vietnamese air force. When we were out in sea, I had an empty feeling in the bottom of my stomach. I looked out at that vast ocean with no land in sight, and I felt like an ant.

What have I done? I thought, feeling completely powerless and helpless.

The captain led the way. Only he knew where to go. We breathed a sigh of relief when we made it to international waters; we knew that the Coast Guard could not attack anyone in free waters. With no compass, the captain followed the moon, sun and stars—and just guessed—to get to our destination. Then we began to realize that we were lost.

Suddenly we heard gunshots. The Coast Guard had seen us and was chasing us, despite our being in the "safety" of international waters.

It was night. A rainstorm had started, making it impossible to see; the enemy was shooting randomly hoping to hit the boat. One motor was shot down. A mechanic on board risked his life to work on the motor while shooting was going on over his head.

This nightmare went on for two hours; then, finally the shooting stopped. We were tired and hungry. The captain acted confident that we were back on track and were headed for Hong Kong—although we did not know for sure. We had run out of fuel, and our only hope was for a wind to blow us in the right direction. Miraculously, the wind came and it did send us the right way. For four more days we traveled without food.

Then we saw land. Like the others, I was elated—my heart beat wildly. But, then fear struck us: We discovered we had landed on an island owned by Red China.

Luck was on our side, though, because, as we later learned, the Red Chinese hated the Vietnam Communists. The Red Chinese fishermen rescued my fellow shipmates and me; they took us to the hospital where we received care. Most of us were unconscious and near death since we had no food or water for such a long time. We lost most of our body weight and were unsure whether our bodies would still function because we were near death. When we awoke, we found ourselves in the hospital and were told all that had happened. We had been extremely lucky—it was a miracle that we were all still alive. None of us died.

Local fishermen repaired the boat for us and gave us fuel, food, a map and a compass. All forty-seven of us again packed like sardines in that small boat made it to Hong Kong two days later.

For two years, we stayed at a refugee camp, and we recovered our health. All refugees had to find a job within two months or their food would be cut off. To get a job, I had to learn how to speak Chinese. During those two years, I worked for a beer factory, a toy factory, an assembler and a machine factory; and, I sent money home to my parents.

After two years, Hong Kong sent me to the Philippines. I tried for months to find my brother-in-law who lived in the United States, but to no avail. I did find a friend, who promised to help me if I came to America. Eventually, in 1981, I made it to the United States.

My struggles did not end, though, with my arrival in Sacramento, California. My friend never met me at the bus stop. I only had $50 in my pocket, and I knew no one and spoke very little English. Homeless, able to afford to eat only one slice of bread a day, I felt like I had reached the bottom. I had no hope. My life was over, I thought.

Then I reflected on all I had been through to that point. I had survived the most inhuman conditions. *I will be able to overcome this, too*, I told myself. After a month in Sacramento, I found a Vietnamese church in the community. The church community befriended me, taught me English, and took me to the local welfare agency to get food stamps. They gave me hope. I survived due to the help of the church.

My first job in America was at Winchell's Donuts. Later, a church member landed me a job as an electrical drafter. On the job, I learned drafting and saved money for college. At Sacramento State University I earned a bachelor's degree in electrical engineering.

My life has progressed so much since those years of flight. Now, I am married; my wife, Nga, and I have a six-year-old boy, Widlar. And, I am currently taking another life adventure by joining a very early stage startup high-tech company in Sunnyvale, California, GuideTech Inc., as a Senior Electronics Test Engineer.

Determination is most important to me. I believe you must be determined to succeed in life. Life is short and we only have one life to live—give it your best. Play hard. Stay focused and never give up. Do your best.

Activity

Dismantling Barriers

How is your will? Can you change yourself when necessary to push onward to the life you want to have? Loc's experience was extreme, but it shows us that there is always a motivating factor that moves us to the next level of action. Try this activity to help you begin meeting one of your goals.

☐ **GOAL:** Below, write one goal you really, really want.

☐ **WHY:** Why is this goal important to you? List your hopes
and expectations below.

☐ **BARRIERS:** What barriers might prevent you from achieving your goal?

☐ **DO:** What will you do to overcome those barriers you identified above? Will you be more assertive and push through your doubts and fears? Can you identify alternatives to allow you to overcome those barriers? Is it something you really want to do? List the barriers below again and dis mantle them so that you can reach your goal.

☐ **ACTION:** What actions can you take to achieve your goal? Can you call a friend or mentor for suggestions, do some brainstorming with friends or coworkers, go back to college, or take some workshops? What else might you do?

☐ Take a look at your action list and begin by doing one thing on it. Promise yourself you will not stop until you accomplish that one task. *Congratulations!*—you have strengthened your will. The more you practice using your will, the easier it will become and you will break down your barriers.

Part II

Boosting Your
Self-Motivation

WE NEED excitement, hope, faith, enthusiasm and other energy boosters to continue on our quest for success. We need ways to continuously reenergize our bodies, minds and souls. Once we learn how to maintain that inner urge of self-motivation, anything is possible.

"Motivation is that which induces action or determines choice,"[6] said Napoleon Hill. The following dynamic stories and activities can advance our dreams and goals by helping us practice self-motivation techniques to persevere even in the tough times. We can break barriers by using self-motivation every day of our lives. Best of all, self-motivation is fun, exciting and invigorating.

Chapter 6

Enthusiasm:
The Greatest
Energy Booster

*"It is the greatest shot of adrenaline
to be doing what you've wanted to do so badly.
You almost feel like
you could fly without the plane."*

—

Charles Lindberg

with Chao Huang

ENTHUSIASM—what a fantastic energy booster!

When you have it you feel like you're soaring. You can complete anything you want because you are in "The Zone"[7]. When you are around others who have zeal, you want to mingle with them in the hope that some of that oomph will rub off on you.

Enthusiasm is infectious—we pass it on to each other. Recently, I was in a restaurant and a lady at the next table began laughing and laughing at something her dinner partner said. Others near her began giggling for no reason at all except that she was laughing. Soon, uncontrollable laughter, giggles and smiles had spread throughout the restaurant. Excitement is important to success—it allows people to attract other people who also want to be successful. Together, they can accomplish more than alone.

Chao Huang, founder of www.joymail.com, affects those around him with his fervor. His way of spreading enthusiasm is through his love for what he is doing today and his willingness to share his ideas with others. With three masters degrees and one doctorate—all accomplished in a six-year period—he entered the Internet world bursting with ideas and zeal.

✳   ✳   ✳

AS Joan and I sat at Coco's Restaurant in Sunnyvale, California, while she interviewed me for her book, my cell phone rang. It was Oliver, one of the founders of ID Star Inc., a company we were about to start. We both became very excited discussing new ideas about that project. Then I realized that Joan would be interested in the issues about startups, so I told Oliver about her and asked if he would share our enthusiasm with her too.

I passed the phone to Joan and she began to talk. We got into a three-way conversation—passing the phone back and forth. In no time at all, we were all surged with energy and having fun as we shared thoughts and ideas. Then suddenly Oliver said, "Wait, we have to do this in person. I will be right there!" That happened at 10:30 P.M. on a Sunday night.

Once you're in this zestful mood, the creative ideas flow nonstop throughout your conversation. We all want this feeling—if we could, we would grab it and keep it forever.

Enthusiasm is not a quality a person just has—it is the culmination of many other experiences and emotions: You must have a fundamental belief and commitments in a cause before you become fervent about it. This cause can be something you passionately want to do or something you earnestly believe in.

I always knew that I wanted to create new products and services. Every time I had an idea, I would write it down and file it. My folders were three inches thick.

Yet, before the Internet, I wasn't always as eager as I am now. When I worked in corporate America on NASA's Star Wars projects, the Star Wars technology challenges kept me at a high level of energy, creativity and interest; but, then, the projects were canceled. Not able to see my contribution in use, I felt disappointed: The challenge was gone, and I quickly became bored. Although I had a lot of ideas, I had nowhere to use them then. I had seen seven or eight company layoffs in my eighteen years on the job, and I was feeling like a temporary contract employee. I began hating my job and found it difficult to keep on going—I was de-motivated and burned out.

Maybe it was fate, but I was doing something right even though I did not know it. I had turned my attention to understanding the stock market and also helped my brother set up the Szechuan Garden Restaurant in Mountain View, California, in 1984. I did all the creative financing—that is, starting it with nothing but eleven credit cards. That seemed very daring at the time with the prime rate as high as 20 percent, but I developed a risk-free scheme and with immediate success with the restaurant we paid off all the money in six months. You can still find the Szechuan Garden on Castro Street—it has run for fifteen years without any advertisement!

I was so proud and confident that one time I proclaimed, "Drop me anyplace in the States and I can start a money-making restaurant." I did not continue that route, however, because in general running a restaurant is a very tough lifestyle. Yet, without realizing it, I had been developing my business skills.

In the mid-1990s, I began seeing exciting opportunities on the Internet for anyone with an idea and a dream. (During that time, Yahoo, Hotmail and LinkExchange were still small startups.) So, in 1996 I quit my job, and soon after began working on my Joymail software project. I ventured into the Internet world in 1997 with **www.joymail.com**, an Internet e-mail provider serving primarily the Chinese community with unique Chinese language entry and display technology on the Web. My newfound love for the Internet rekindled my zeal.

Enthusiasm is fundamentally important to the success of a venture. People wanted to work for free as interns on the Joymail project: These innovative people would work long hours just to learn something new; they were fueled with eagerness at the opportunity of being part of the Internet world. I gave them a chance to use their creativity to develop new ideas and learn the Internet market. They, too, had been bored at their corporate jobs— they took the leap and accepted those new challenges together with me.

Failure is just a mistake or a temporary wrong turn: We try over again, correct what we're doing, and move on from there. Enthusiasm gives me supreme confidence. When I have an idea, I can delay it—but eventually I have to do it. Do what you love to do. Keep challenging yourself.

When we are passionate about what we are doing, our positive energy field passes on to others within our reach, including those who hear our voice over the telephone. We might even spread it via a message on the Internet. We feel our excitement and so do the people around us. When we have enthusiasm, others want it, and they will stay with us so that they can continue to experience that positive energy, which is actually a feeling of mild ecstasy. And, when we have this feeling, we can do anything. We have supreme confidence in our abilities and are totally immersed in what we are doing.

In hindsight, I clearly see what happened to me. I've been creating new things through my love. I had delayed the process—but eventually I had to do it. Do the things you passionately love: That is how you get and keep your enthusiasm.

Rekindling Enthusiasm

You may want to share the following activity with a friend or in a group brainstorming session. A small group of enthusiastic people can reinforce your own belief system and help you stay on target to accomplish your tasks at hand.

1. Name someone you know who embodies enthusiasm.

2. What do you admire about this person?

3. Can you ask this person to be your mentor and spend some time with you?

4. Name some ways you can maintain your zeal.

5. How can you share your excitement with others?

6. How can you encourage others to share their enthusiasm with you?

Activity 2

Rekindling Enthusiasm

1. Describe a situation or time in your life when you just plain lacked enthusiasm.

2. To what did you attribute your lack of zest?

3. What did you do to rekindle your interest?

4. What idea did you get from Chao's story that could help you regain your enthusiasm?

Chapter 7
Trust Begins
With You

"Trust men and they will be true to you;
treat them greatly and they will
show themselves great."

—

Ralph Waldo Emerson

with Dave Latner

DAVE Latner, a former vice president in risk management, had a dream of traveling around the world. In his soft-spoken voice, he described that it was time to "recharge his batteries." But he was not a risk taker. Single and with no commitments, he felt that traveling around the world would be a low-risk experience. All the same, he was both excited and terrified about traveling for an extended time. Hence, his tactic: "I told as many people as I could that I was going to be a world traveler so it would prevent me from backing out."

With his passport, a few clothes, and a healthy amount of anxiety, he took off to a world unknown to him. Soon, he began depending on total strangers that he met along the way—he learned about trusting others.

✻   ✻   ✻

AFTER nineteen countries, four continents, the better part of a year, and intestinal parasites, as well as planes, trains, rickshaws and a lot of adventure, I still am in travel mode. The only way I can overcome my denial of being settled and back in San Francisco is to make a public announcement that I am home—and perhaps, God forbid, venture off to that American icon McDonald's for a Big Mac. So, this right now is my public announcement.

I learned that traveling is easy and you do not necessarily need to know the language of the country you're visiting to get by (although a few words do help). In the Ukraine, where few people spoke English, I discovered how to ask for such things as soap, shampoo and toilet paper through pantomime and exaggerated gestures. Travel tip: When you need toilet paper, it's best to pretend you are blowing your nose and accept facial tissue.

During my travels, trust began to play a big role in my life.

Through friends, I had the names of strangers in New Zealand whom I could call for guidance there. When I reached Australia, I began calling my friends' friends. At first, I felt uncomfortable, but soon I had new friends, places to stay and tour guides for those "off the beaten path" sites that only locals know. I used the Internet to connect with friends at home and to communicate with contacts at my subsequent destinations. Computers with Internet connections were available not only in the big cities, but also in remote villages in Nepal and Indonesia. I could alleviate homesickness with just a few mouse clicks and some rupees or other local currency. I felt connected with my friends in the United States through e-mail.

In the Ukraine, at first I felt the indifference of people—the locals didn't seem to care about a tourist at all. Yet, I believed in serendipity. I went to a local museum where the docents kept trying to explain the exhibits in their native language, assuming that if they repeated themselves and spoke loudly I would eventually understand (a practice I'm embarrassed to admit I have been guilty of in my own country). Not much progress was made, and after twenty minutes, a Ukrainian college student came to my rescue. She translated for the docents, which pleased them because they were proud of their museum and exhibits. The student befriended me and invited me to her friend's art studio for lunch.

The day before, I had read an article about twenty-six people who went blind from drinking homemade alcohol. Here I was in this art studio with my newfound Ukrainian friends, eating lunch and drinking homemade Vodka. I'm happy to say that I survived the visit. I much more than survived: In fact I was in awe at the great hospitality these art friends gave me. They gave me a king's welcome in the most humble surroundings I had seen so far.

I gained faith that people are gentle and kind.

In central Turkey I met a young man waiting for a bus. No one around spoke English, so I wasn't sure of the fare. I boarded the bus but I didn't have the right change. Kindly, the young man paid my fare even though he didn't know me at all.

There were little acts of kindness all along the way by people who did not speak English: One shared a taxi with me. Another gave me a sandwich. We communicated using positive gestures, smiles, and body language. Sure, some people looked at me and "saw" dollar signs exuding from a "Rich American," but I managed to steer clear of those people and had no difficulty finding people who genuinely wanted to help me.

By the time I returned to the United States, I was a different person. I decided to settle in San Francisco where I could take public transportation and continue to meet people. Today, I allow myself the time to walk and meet people. It is easy to fall back into old habits; to avoid one of mine, I locked my television in the closet so that I would have more time to do other things. I keep my car parked in the garage and only use it for emergencies and activities that have time constraints.

I know I have grown from this experience: I recognize that I can easily do things even though they may be uncomfortable for me. Traveling also has helped me with my communication skills. I am more assertive and direct now. I ask for what I want.

Returning home was bittersweet. When I am at the airport, homesickness seems to disappear just like a toothache does in the dentist's waiting room. I am happy to have had the opportunity to travel in the past year; and now here I am—renting an undersized, overpriced apartment in the city I love and eating a Big Mac.

✦

Balancing Your Life

Attempt to do something nice for someone every day. Pay attention and listen to your loved ones. Do something that takes you outside of yourself and does not directly benefit you. Enjoy the act of giving: You could give new stuffed teddy bears to a children's home, or help paint the house of a friend or a neighbor. Join your favorite nonprofit group and become involved. For example, participate in a literacy reading group to help others learn to read. Find other opportunities to help people.

1. Some things I would like to do:

2. The one activity listed above I will do first.

3. I will begin this activity on the following date:

Chapter 8
Timid as a Mouse
No More!

"I believe that anyone can conquer fear by doing the things he fears to do, provided he keeps doing them until he gets a record of successful experiences behind him."

—

Eleanor Roosevelt

with Joan Clout-Kruse

SHYNESS and social anxiety can prevent people from being all they want to be. If you suffer from timidity, you are not alone: Many famous people have dealt with problems of shyness, including Eleanor Roosevelt, Robert Frost and Albert Einstein.[8] They conquered their reticence and contributed greatly to our world. U. S. News and World Report states that social anxiety "is the third most common mental disorder in the United States, behind depression and alcoholism."[9]

Timid people often are very sensitive people with great empathy and good intuition, which makes them great friends once they finally make a connection with someone they feel they can trust. Next time someone avoids you at a party, recognize that they might simply be bashful.

"Shyness is a set of learned behaviors that interfere with relating to people or having successful relationships,"[10] states Nancy Wesson, Ph.D. Fortunately, shy people can also learn to change these behaviors—the secret is that they must want to change. Some experience they have will drive them to alter their ways of relating; they must be propelled into a burning desire to transform and learn new ways to cope with their shyness. Then, they must take the steps to do it.

If you are as reticent as a mouse, or have friends who face this challenge, the following story shows that, as Dr. Wesson states, shyness is indeed a learned behavior and the person can learn to modify that behavior. I promise you that, with practice, anyone can manage and tackle their diffidence. I know for certain—because it happened to me.

Joan Clout-Kruse

✳   ✳   ✳

ONE day when I was in the Ninth Grade at Horace Mann Junior High School in San Francisco, I stood behind the lectern ready to speak to the entire student body on why they should vote for me for student body secretary. I looked out at the audience and panicked. It seemed like a thousand students were staring at me, waiting for me to speak. My hands became clammy, perspiration ran down my forehead and my knees and hands shook. I pressed my notes tightly against the lectern so no one would see how nervous I was. I wondered, *Why did I ever agree to do this?*

Making posters had been fun: One of them read, "Behind Every Clout There's a Silver Lining!" A creative friend and I had a grand time drawing the posters and hanging them in the hallways of the school. I was positive those posters would elect me. They looked so professional. I expected to win the election. But, that was before I stood behind the lectern that day: It was no fun at all—rather it was the worst day of my life. I read my notes as fast as I could, and sat down—my hands and knees were still shaking.

On that day, I promised myself one thing: *I will never speak in front of a group again!* I meant it. Do you know the old saying, "Watch out what you ask for because you might get it"? Well that's what happened to me. After that day, I avoided any kind of public speaking. To evade it, I went as far as keeping my eyes down in class so the teacher wouldn't call on me and even avoiding eye contact when I walked down a street for fear a stranger might talk to me, or—heaven forbid—smile at me!

My shyness was debilitating. I could only meet new people if they took the first step to introduce themselves. I disliked social events. In junior high, where we were required to take a coed dance class, I was your classic wallflower; if a guy walked towards me to ask me to dance, I would get an anxious stomach. Most girls had a fear that they wouldn't be asked to dance. I was afraid that I would be asked to dance! In general, if I had to meet someone I didn't know, I felt such fear that my heart would beat wildly, my hands would sweat, and my mind would become blank at the mere thought.

In my early years, I thought I was the only one with this issue, and I endured this anxiety phobia into my twenties and thirties. I could function normally—well, that is, I could succeed personally and in my career as long as I did not have to talk in front of a group, meet new people, or attend social events or parties! I had many accomplishments, but the time came when my shyness was holding me back. I had to face the reality that in order to be promoted and reach more of my aims in life, I had to overcome my timid behavior. I needed to transform and become more sociable with people, even though just thinking about it brought shivers of fear inside me. I set a goal to learn to cope with my reticence, become more aware of opportunities to meet people, and do it!

The event that motivated me to confront my problem and precipitated my turning point came the day I did not receive a promotion I expected—someone else got it; a friend and co-worker who I knew very well. I asked myself what he had that I didn't have: We both had the same qualifications and experience. Yet I swiftly realized the answer: he had charisma and enthusiasm, and he enjoyed himself at social events. He was fun to be around.

I decided to take action. The first step I took to triumph over my social anxiety, was enrolling in The Dale Carnegie Course® on "Effective Speaking." This program taught me how to manage my anxious moments. All forty of us at the first session, each had to introduce ourselves in two minutes time. My usual fear of speaking overwhelmed me that day. As I waited for my turn, my heart was beating so hard that I thought I would have a heart attack. The first thing I noticed was that there were others who had similar fears. One lady almost broke into tears as she gave her two-minute introduction. She became one of the best speakers, at the end of the 14-week program. When it came my turn to speak, I managed to get through it hoping I would not have to do it again. However, I soon learned that every week we would each be giving a two-minute speech on the subject for that week. We were learning human relations' skills, which helped me to understand others, and also how to communicate in any social or business setting. My favorite was, "Don't criticize, condemn or complain." I was always challenging myself to find the good in people whom I met after learning that phrase. It became a game and it was fun to do. Because of the support of the Instructor and the encouragement of my fellow classmates, each speech I gave got easier and easier. In time, I eventually looked forward to speaking. I was amazed at how much all of us had progressed over the 14 weeks. At our last session, we were ready to "conquer our world!"

Another management workshop I took later suggested that I set a goal to introduce myself to five strangers at each social event I would attend. To this day, I promise myself to meet that goal whenever I go to a social occasion. However, it continues to call for my conscious effort; it doesn't come naturally. I could easily sink back into my introvert mode anytime I want, and must remain aware that I have to "work" the room.

Today, I love to speak in front of groups—I love to share my ideas and help others. I also overcame that dreaded "guy might ask me to dance" fear long ago. I met my husband, Don, at a singles dance I attended all by myself at the YMCA. I have come a long way, and so can you even if now you are timid as a mouse. The first step to transformation is that you really want to change.

Remember my Ninth Grade fear-of-speaking debacle? I actually won the student body secretary position! It was just a few years ago that I recalled I had won that election. In all these years I only focused on my embarrassing speaking moment. I had totally erased from my mind that I had a success that day. Isn't it strange how I promised never to speak in public again even after I won? This awakening taught me that we must pay more attention to our successes, learn from our mistakes and fears, and just move on.

Strengthening Your Boldness

Does your shyness hold you back from achieving the successes you want in your life? If so, are you willing to alter your behavior? Listed below are some activities that can help you manage your shyness. Go slow—at your own pace—but do try some of them. Remember that usually your reticence will be there with you. You have to be mindful at all times that you want to make a change. Ask a friend along to any of the activities listed below if you feel it would be too difficult to do alone.

☐ Take a speaking course at your local community college.

☐ Take a drama class at your local community college.

☐ Do volunteer work for your favorite charity. You will make new friends and build your self-esteem as you learn new skills.

☐ Take the Dale Carnegie® Training program on "Effective Speaking." For more information, review their Web site: www.dalecarnegie.com.

☐ Visit and join a Toastmasters International® club in your area. The clubs have a structured program on public speaking and communication skills, including constructive evaluation, to help members learn how to talk with others and manage their fears. For locations of a club near you, check their Web site at www.toastmasters.org.

☐ Next time you are at a social event, introduce yourself to five strangers. If it feels too threatening to you, ask an extroverted friend to introduce you to five strangers—but do not let your friend take over the conversation. In order to learn you must be involved.

☐ Collect business cards or write down the names, addresses and phone numbers of the people you meet. Repeat their names as you're introduced to help you remember the names. Find out something about them—for example, their hobbies, job or their family members. People do like having an interest shown in them. Enjoy getting to know each one of them; you may find you share something in common.

☐ Always be kind to yourself. Maintain a positive attitude towards yourself and avoid critical self-talk.

Chapter 9
Stuck? Find a Buddy
and Commit!

"Together we can achieve the extraordinary"

—

unknown

with Marc Isaac Potter

ARE you still hesitant to try some of the activities suggested in this book? You can become "unstuck" by learning to break old patterns and reinvent yourself: In other words, alter your behavior. To do this, you must practice the "art of commitment"—commitment is one of the traits most important to advance you to your goals. Once you learn how to keep a promise to yourself and others, you will probably feel as though you're taking in a breath of fresh air.

Marc Isaac Potter conceptualized a workbook to help others learn how to commit and manage procrastination in their lives, but the actual writing of the book became an unanticipated challenge.

✳   ✳   ✳

I N June of 1996, after years of yearning to be an effective leader of communication seminars, I began writing my workbook. I wrote for weeks, but then I simply could not finish it. In despair, I threw the entire manuscript in the trash and began writing about a different subject. Three-fourths of the way into this second project I froze up again—I was stuck. This was a classic case of "writer's block."

I hit the impasse again the next time I started to write. My patience was waning: I wanted to get over my writer's block now. At this point, I was at my wits' end. *There must be a way for me to finish this workbook,* I thought.

The concept of my workbook was "acquiring support from others to accomplish your goals." It dawned on me that I needed to actualize the purpose of this workbook—to commit and achieve with the support of a colleague. I knew that my friend Joan Clout-Kruse had experience at writing manuals; I decided to ask her to work with me on the book.

Joan agreed to work with me. We began meeting weekly in the beginning and worked closely for several months completing the workbook together, sharing ideas and support. Upon completion of the book, we became co-authors and workshop leaders of a program entitled, *The Secrets of Cooperative Agreements.* Eventually we obtained the trademark for the name *Cooperative Agreements*®.

Cooperative Agreements Partner Program (CAPP) is all about working, supporting and learning together to make our dreams a reality. With the buddy system as described in this chapter, you make formal agreements with another to accomplish each task. That is the key: formal agreements. This is not an informal "meet with a friend once in a while and try to do what needs to be done" kind of thing. When using the buddy system, or CAPP as it is called, the partners are committed. We met regularly and sent e-mail messages to each other to report on our progress with the goals we set for completing the manual. Each of us listed the next step we would take to meet our individual goals. At our next meeting we reported on our accomplishments (or the lack thereof) related to the specific task we had targeted.

Sometimes our meetings were excruciatingly painful as we learned new things together—such as how to trademark a name and how to market the seminars. Working together, we pushed ourselves to complete the task. We rarely procrastinated because we were dedicated to accomplishing certain assignments during the week and reporting on the results at our next meeting. We learned the real meaning of commitment. When we said yes, we meant it. We avoided words like "try," "maybe," or "should." The more we met, the easier it became to keep a promise.

The benefits of working with a partner on my workbook were many: It calmed my nervousness. I gained a new kind of accountability. I received practical information about how to proceed and how to improve what I had written, and my buddy actually did some of the work that I felt I could not do. Also, my partner was a good listener.

The CAPP concept can speed your progress towards achieving your goal, allowing you to bypass many of the obstacles that come your way. Your buddy can help you move through tough times and mental blocks by encouraging you to persist in your endeavors. For this to work, you must have a trustworthy friend, mentor or colleague who is willing to talk and/or meet with you on a regular basis. The person can not have a secondary agenda that would interfere with you working well together.

The CAPP workbook highlights five key elements that each partner must have for this cooperative system to work: self-reliance, support, cooperation, willingness and trust.

The CAPP concept does work. It is a formal agreement program, which requires a written commitment from both of you to meet willingly and communicate regularly to share your goals and dreams with each other. The written agreement is a way of emotionally preparing for the work you will embark on together. Anytime either one of you wants to quit, you can.

If your buddy has the key element characteristics listed above, your visions and theirs can become a reality. Other people can assist you in fulfilling your dreams. Find that special person to be your buddy, and if you both promise to follow a mutually agreed upon plan, you can shift and progress.

✳

Rekindling Commitment

Listed below is an abbreviated version of the Cooperative Agreements®
Partner Program. Try out this concept of committing with your partner to
meet regularly and set specific tasks to complete each week or two to reach
your goal. If you fail to finish the task before the agreed-upon time, revise
the agreement with your buddy. They should be a good listener and neither
criticize nor condemn you if you do not meet your agreement. You just move
on with your task from that point, form a new agreement and persevere.

The buddy system can work for both people engaged in this agreement.
You and your partner can each be working on a separate goal. Report weekly or bi-weekly how you are doing, and support each other. Remember to
have empathy and remain positive with your buddy if he or she does not meet
the goal for that date. Remake the agreement and move on from there. Get
moving again—get a buddy!

COOPERATIVE AGREEMENTS ACTION PLAN

Action Step 1: *Create a Right Attitude*

Decide with your buddy whether you each will work on the same goal or
independent goals. Use a notebook and label it "Agreement Book"; keep all
your notes in it. Your partner should also use a notebook for note writing and
keeping track of affirmed agreements.
Be sure the goals are things you really want!

Goal(s): _____

_____

_____

_____

_____

_____

Agreements: Below, write a positive, affirmative statement like "I will do this." Don't write "I will try to do this." You are making an agreement with your partner that you will accomplish particular tasks.

_____
_____
_____
_____

Action Step 2: *Make a Commitment*

Both parties must arrive at a common understanding as to what each is agreeing to do. Remember, the agreements you make show your skill of cooperation and increase your self-reliance.

What would you like your partner to do to help you reach your goal?

_____
_____
_____

What are you willing to do to achieve your goal?

_____
_____
_____

Action Step 3: *Be Clear and Concise*

Agreements must have enough detail to address each part of the under standing. Avoid assumptions! Map out the tasks you must perform to meet your goal by using milestone markers.

List the major steps to reach your goal.

_____
_____
_____
_____
_____

Action Step 4: *Be Specific*

Agreements work best when the commitment is made very specific. One way to empower the contract is to put a deadline on the items, specifically a date and time of day when you will complete each action. For example: "I will call you by 3:30 P.M. every Friday." Commitments must be very specific.
Below, write the steps that you listed in Step 3, and add a deadline for achieving each step.

Action Step 5: *Declare it!*

Agreements become powerful when they are declared. Pronouncing your agreement in a clear and direct tone empowers you to fulfill your commitment. Declarations can be written or verbal.

Announce your commitment to each other. Example:

Partner A: "I will walk on Monday, Wednesday, Friday and Saturday for at least thirty minutes beginning at 6:30 A.M."

Partner B: "I will support you in walking by coming over on Monday and Friday at 6:30 A.M. I will walk with you for thirty minutes. If I cannot come over, I will call as soon as I know I can't make it, and I will make that walking period up within five days."

Sign or Shake Hands
If the agreement is written, then each of you signs the agreement. If the agreement is verbal, shake hands. If either of you is uncomfortable about doing this, explore together what the problem is and how you can solve it.

The Results:

When you complete this program with your partner, you will have enhanced your commitment, trust, self-reliance and cooperative skills. Also, you will have decreased one of the greatest energy drainers, dream stealers, and ambition stealers we experience: *procrastination.*

———————————

The above program is an adapted version from the workbook *The Secrets of Cooperative Agreements* ©1997 by Marc Isaac Potter and Joan Clout-Kruse.

Chapter 10
Hope is the
Mainspring in Life

*"Hope works in these ways:
it looks for the good in people instead of
harping on the worst; it discovers what can be
done instead of grumbling about what cannot;
it regards the problems, large or small, as
opportunities; it pushes ahead when it would
be easy to quit; it 'lights the candle' instead
of 'cursing the darkness.'"*

—

Anon

with Kilsoon Kim *and daughter* Jinsoo Terry

THIS is the story of Kilsoon Kim, an amazing Korean woman who persevered although it seemed there was no way through. When a barrier appeared, she looked for a way around and never gave up hope. She looked for the positive side of people, saw difficulties as challenges, and always looked for people who could help her fulfill her goals. It is also the story of Kilsoon's daughter, Jinsoo Terry, who lived her mother's aspirations for her.

✳   ✳   ✳

Kilsoon Kim

It was 1947, when I was a teenager; my parents told me to flee North Korea because the government had stripped citizens of all of their rights. My father owned the first private post office in the city—and he was about to lose it.

"Go, Kilsoon!" my father said anxiously, "We will follow you tomorrow after your brother comes home." I left my parents, brothers and sisters behind and fled to South Korea to stay with a sister who was already there. I never saw or heard from my parents, brothers or sisters again. To this day, I do not know what happened to them.

I was a budding opera singer in North Korea and carried a music teacher's certificate with me to South Korea. I was soon able to get a job teaching music, singing and piano in an elementary school. Eventually, I married a middle school teacher and over time we had three children.

Jinsoo was the firstborn. Her birth name was Jinhee, a girl's name; however, one day I met a Monk outside my door and he told me to change my daughter's first name to "Jinsoo" because my daughter would have more opportunities with a boy's name. I changed her name and from that moment on I felt she was destined for great things.

In 1979, with my three children in college—Jinsoo studying to be an engineer—everything seemed to be going well. But then tragedy struck, my husband died. The sadness became greater because the only way I could keep the children in college was by selling the house. After discussing it with my children, I decided to sell the house—my last item of security. Times grew difficult and even worse as we struggled in near poverty; yet, I was driven by the belief that educated children have a better chance in life. I was determined that my children would receive a college education. I never looked back.

In 1982, Jinsoo gained her engineering degree but could not acquire a job because she was a woman "in a man's world." I encouraged her to continue and earn her master's degree. "Don't give up. You will get an engineering job with a master's degree," I reassured Jinsoo.

Jinsoo Terry continues:

My mother never taught me how to clean a house. She encouraged me to study and learn. She was always there for me; she's been my best friend. Her love, faith and hope were always forthcoming. My mother said that men have the best jobs, so I should "go to college with the men." But I was afraid of men.

She would say, "If you want to catch a tiger, you have to go to the tiger's cave. You must go to college where the men go."

It was now 1984. With a second degree in hand I still could not obtain work. I felt like a failure. No employment, and my mother was $40,000 in debt. My life is finished, I thought.

On one sunny day I still remember clearly, my mother said, "Don't give up. Why don't you move to Seoul? They have greater opportunities." I was taken aback when my mother handed me $900 that she had saved. She gave it to me to embark on getting my doctorate degree. I was very impressed and I cried when I saw it, knowing the sacrifice she must have made to save that money. I told her I can't spend the money, but she insisted that I take it. While I was working on my doctorate, mom called friends of hers from her early teaching days to tell them that I was looking for an engineer's job. She passed along the word wherever she could. Never lowering her standards, she expected me to land an engineer's job. After I learned that textile manufacturing was a major industry in Korea, I pursued a degree in yarn dyeing.

My mother delivered my resumé to every textile company in the area. It paid off! She found me a textile job while I was in graduate school. I started out as the lowest-paid employee in a male-dominated company. Then, one propitious day the company opened one of the biggest yarn-dyeing factories in Korea, and the president of the company discovered that I was an expert in this field.

On that one day I jumped from the lowest-paid employee to one of the highest-paid employees in the company. I was given a top position as director of research and development. At twenty-eight, I was directing a department of male engineers—just as my mother had envisioned.

A few years later when I was at a party, I met Sam, a traveling American. The first time I introduced my mother to Sam, she knew "he was the one." She felt it, knew it. Destiny had touched me again.

Today I live in Berkeley, California, with my husband Sam. I am the director of manufacturing for a well-known clothing manufacturer in San Francisco.

Mom is an expert on confidence. She motivated and encouraged me and my brother and sister to do our best and always believe in ourselves. Today, my sister is an opera singer and high school music teacher in Korea. My brother owns his own business. All three of us purchased a three-bedroom home in Seoul for our mother.

Kilsoon Kim

Cultivate a vision and don't look back. Follow your dreams. Never give up hope. Let go of any negativity in your past and look for the good in people. Allow people to help you attain your aspirations; ask for help and tell others what you want. You can make your wishes a reality. Success is doing whatever you want to do.

Today I travel around the world to see my many friends in other countries. I am following my vision better and I am happy knowing that my children are following theirs too.

Activity

Keeping Hope Alive

How do you keep hope alive during the tough times? When there seems to be "no light at the end of the tunnel," how do you cope?

Prepare yourself. Listed below are some activities you can do to keep hope alive. Make one (√) checkmark by the ones that you do regularly. Put two checkmarks (√√) by those you need to work on. Take those activities and practice them everyday.

☐ I can **yank** myself out of the doldrums by saying, "I can always find a way." I will say this as often as needed.

☐ I will create an **Accomplishment Book** and write all the positive mile stones that happened in my life. Periodically I will review my book, especially on tough days. I will practice positive thinking and keep a good attitude.

☐ I will keep **aware** each day of what is going on in my life at that moment. When I notice that I am slipping into a feeling of hopelessness, I will "snap out of it" by calling a friend.

☐ I will **laugh** and be joyful each day, as laughter heals. I will smile many times each day as I greet people.

☐ I will find a way to get **help** and support immediately from a trusted friend, pastor, support group or a professional therapist.

☐ I will find a way to **overcome** any **obstacles** that come my way.

☐ I will **pray** or **meditate**, as it will help me to stay focused on solving my problems and will keep me mentally healthy and alert. My daily prayers will keep my faith strong.

Above excerpts taken from the booklet, *Keep Hope Alive*, ©2000 by Joan Clout-Kruse.

73

Part III
Building Your
New Life Plan

THE ONLY WAY to get what we want is to go for it—no matter what it takes! We have learned in Parts I and II how to break through barriers and reenergize ourselves with self-motivation. Now it is time to actually do it—no excuses.

The achievers in the following stories show us how they pursued their goals. They will share ideas that worked for them: visualizing, networking, planning, rekindling a dream and creating a new dream. The time to act is now!

Chapter 11
Build Your
Network

"A Key to Success is not who you know.
It's who knows YOU!"

—

Cesar Plata

with Cesar Plata

WHO do you know that can help you achieve your goals? Who do you contact to bounce off your ideas? Who knows enough about you to help you get what you want?

One person I know, Cesar Plata, is blazing trails in helping people connect with each other: Through his Web site **www.muybueno.net**, Cesar has developed an amazing network that informs and helps unite thousands of predominantly Bay Area Latino professionals, including many corporate, government and community leaders. From mechanical engineer to entrepreneur, this pioneer is pursuing his dream.

✶   ✶   ✶

I had envisioned creating a hub to unite the Bay Area Latino professional community; this would provide a nucleus of information on events and resources related to business, community, culture, education, and entertainment. In addition to achieving this dream, I also host monthly professional socials to promote unity, business, education and leadership. These networking opportunities reduce exclusivity with the community because everyone is invited to become involved and join forces to work together. I also help promote underrepresented businesses and organizations to do business with each other, thus helping to develop the financial growth and empowerment of our community.

I realized that if more people became aware of the events taking place and the opportunities available to involve themselves in community activities—especially the mentoring of our youth—our community would naturally grow stronger and more united. We would also see a rise in the graduation rates of minority students.

This aspiration began as a hobby back in 1996. Initially, my service consisted of a weekly e-mail list of events, activities and resources that I believed would be of interest to several hundred of my friends, colleagues and acquaintances. By 1997, my hobby and idea had gained a substantial following throughout the Bay Area Latino community. In late 1998 I decided to pursue my dream of becoming an entrepreneur by transforming my hobby into a full-time business. Throughout 1999, I formed substantial partnerships with key organizations and businesses all over California. With the help of my friend Rhéal Paquette we designed and launched our Web site **www.muybueno.net**. Gradually, media sources and, most importantly, word of mouth, have helped promote **www.muybueno.net**.

I recognized that people need to connect, not only online, but also in person, to enhance their opportunities for personal and business success. Hundreds of people regularly attend the monthly professional socials in San Jose and San Francisco. These are great venues to socialize with your peers, meet corporate and community leaders, and make new friends and business contacts in a friendly, fun, and comfortable environment. I truly believe the best business is personal business. People are more likely to do business with you if they feel comfortable with you and appreciate the services you provide. I also help several mentoring organizations by providing them with a list of more than a thousand professionals who have registered to volunteer as mentors, public speakers, workshop presenters and as board members of nonprofit organizations.

From personal experience, I recognized how important it is for people to share their goals, aspirations and resources with others. Associate yourself with success-oriented and positive people, and they will encourage and help you to succeed.

So far, several television and radio stations, as well as newspapers and magazines have featured muybueno.net and the monthly socials. Best of all, people promote **www.muybueno.net** by talking to each other about it. To date, my list of subscribers has grown to more than eight thousand. **www.muybueno.net** has surfaced as a true virtual and real community of professionals and leaders throughout the Bay Area.

As with anyone launching a startup business, I have endured many personal and financial sacrifices and struggles. I did not see these efforts as barriers; I accepted them as learning experiences. The way I see it, they were simply unmet challenges.

I strongly believe that a key to success is not what you know, or who you know, but who knows you! Following are a few comments submitted to the online guestbook that reinforce the concept that "it's who knows you that matters."

"Cesar, I would like to thank you very much for your help with finding contact people and employers willing to provide summer jobs to our students. Ultimately, I was able to place all 60 students who

*qualified for the summer jobs program. Thank you again and I wish
you well with all your great projects!"*

> Tony S.,
> Industry Liaison, East Side Union High School District,
> San Jose, California

*"The socials have brought us new business already. Your efforts to
bring the community together are great!"*

> Pamela D.,
> Ideal Power Promotion,
> Manteca, California

*"Last August we approached Cesar regarding an under-
privileged youth at our school who desperately needed a bike. Cesar
invited us to attend the San Jose Social and inform others of our
situation. Several guests showed interest, and one of the event's
sponsors from Allstate encouraged others to take note. So now
thanks to three gentlemen who offered to buy Carlos a bike, getting
to and from school is no longer an issue for Carlos. Thank you to all
who responded, and especially to Cesar for allowing us to use this
venue. The five of you served as 'angels' for Carlos, and this gesture
will stay in our hearts."*

> Elida A.,
> San Jose, California

Make a name for yourself and let your reputation precede you. Enjoy
what you do, do what is right, follow your passion, believe in yourself, and
help yourself so you may in turn help others. The rewards will far exceed
your efforts!

Developing Your Network of Contacts

Just as Cesar did, create your own list of contacts. Identify several positive, encouraging people who can help you get what you want.

1. Who in your circle of friends can help you achieve your goals? Identify why you think they can help. Be specific about how you might use their assistance. Knowing what their expertise is will be helpful to you.

_____

_____

_____

2. Who in your circle of colleagues, coworkers and other professional contacts can help you achieve your goals? These may be people you don't know but whom you think could help.

_____

_____

_____

3. Telephone the people listed above and ask for their help. Meet with them; share your ideas. Listen to their dreams and ideas, too. You may be amazed to see how the mutual support and respect you share with other constructive people can help you fulfill your goals. Let them tell you if they can help.

4. Start small with five names, and eventually increase your list until it's between 25 and 50 names of people you have personally contacted. One person said, "I don't know that many people whom I feel comfortable talking to. In fact, I don't even have ten names on my list." If that reflects your situation, I suggest you join some community organizations such as Rotary Club, Chamber of Commerce, Toastmasters, and the Optimists Club. Find out about other clubs in your community, too. Become actively involved in your community and get to know the people in it—in time you will have a list of 50- plus superachievers who would love to help you reach your dreams; and you, in turn, will help and support their dreams.

Chapter 12
Share Your
Passion

*"Successful people love to help others
achieve their dreams. Ask for help"*

—

Gail Turner

with Gail Turner

GAIL Turner—a mother, grandmother, teacher, business woman, and professional speaker—built two airplanes, owned a hard-chrome-plating manufacturing company, and raised and trained Apaloosa horses. Each achievement began with a dream that she envisioned and then acted upon, carving out her own opportunities. With passionate tenacity, she turned her aspirations into reality. She was the first woman to build and fly solo her own aircraft from California to Oshkosh, Wisconsin, which led to her being featured in Newsweek *and* Time *magazines and in many TV documentaries. Today she is vice president of corporate solutions for J. Paul Bagan & Associates, presenting The Dale Carnegie Training course.*

Gail succeeded in her ambitions by sharing her dreams and by asking others for help when she needed it. These are her five keys to success:

1.   Visualize what you want to have happen. You don't have to know how to get there. Just think it, feel it, taste it, want it and see it in your mind's eye. We attract into our lives that on which we focus.

2.   Apply bulldog tenacity to whatever you are going to do. Grab, hold and don't let go.

3.   Don't be afraid to ask for help. Get advice: Successful people love to help others actualize their dreams.

4.   Share your passion. Give back. Be an encourager.

5.   Maintain a positive attitude toward risk and adventure.

✳   ✳   ✳

IN the '70s I had a burning desire to build an airplane. At first my pilot friends teased me and said that a woman—"especially a Kindergarten teacher!"—couldn't build a plane. That was exactly the motivation I needed to commit myself to doing it. I wanted to do something unique, something that no woman had done before, even though I knew nothing about building airplanes and was very new at flying them.

I built my first plane in the living room of my Belmont, California, home in 1975—airplane parts strewn in every room of the house. The good news was that I didn't have to clean house. My girlfriends helped me drill holes, glue fabric to wooden wing ribs and iron the fabric to take out the wrinkles. From my Kindergartener's standpoint, it was a big cut-and-paste project. The Fly Baby was economical with her 65 horsepower Contimal Engine that used only four gallons an hour. Her wing folded up so I could keep her at home in the garage: No hangar costs. Fortunately, we didn't know "we couldn't do it," that we couldn't build an airplane in the house. It was a Pete Bower's "Fly Baby" design, low wing monoplane, all wood and fabric. I painted the fuselage bright hot pink with black lace crosses on the wings and called it "The Pink Baroness"; I wanted everyone to know that it was "woman built." In a short fourteen months she was flying: The average time for a home built plane is twelve years.

In July 1977 the Fly Baby and I were off to Oshkosh, Wisconsin, "the air show of all air shows" sponsored by the Experimental Aircraft Association. Time magazine and Newsweek gave us coverage. Peoples' positive reaction to my funny little pink airplane was overwhelming and very gratifying.

After nine tail-tiring days of flying low and slow (averaging 75 miles per hour—even Volkswagen cars were passing us when they went downhill—I discovered that the Fly Baby was limited in performance. I became itchy to do flip-flops in the sky like the rest of my nutty friends. So I began searching again for my dream machine. Finding none that I could afford, that inner urge to build a plane arose in me again for my second plane. I decided on a Marquart M5 Charger plane—an open cockpit Biplane. It had 10° swept wings and four ailerons with which I would do wonderful rolls and lazy "8's" in the azure skies.

Once again I learned the true value of surrounding myself with talented people. I asked for help and got it. My friends supported my new dream and helped me with everything from applying Polyfiber, rigging wings, stitching all the panels, masking, painting, plumbing the engine and much more.

In 1979, after devoting 3-1/2 years of my life to my vision, I took off on my first solo flight in my radiant yellow, red and orange biplane. What an indescribable thrill to realize that my vast collection of bits and pieces, stitches and rivets, and sweat and tears had finally come together into the beautiful airplane that I called "Duchess Papillon"—The Butterfly.

I could not have built my airplanes without the assistance and advice of others. Although I didn't know it when I began building the second plane, I was way over my head. Don't be afraid to ask for support. People will assist you if you share your dreams sincerely and with passion. More than thirty people helped me build my second plane. Others like to be a part of your journey to succeed—learn how to make them a part of your dream.

My successes at building and flying two airplanes propelled my self-esteem to an all-time high: I believed I could do anything. I was yearning to leave teaching Kindergarten and create my own business. I started calling people who ran their own business and asked them what to do. One of my calls was to a friend who had a manufacturing plant, and he suggested I start a hard-chrome-plating service. I said okay, not even knowing what hard-chrome-plating was! None of us can have success without taking risks. I had to step out and try something new even if I didn't know what the outcome would be. Even though there were rough times, there were no failures, only *outcomes* on which I could improve.

From 1980 to 1988, I ran my own company, L. G. Turner Hard Chrome Plating, which plated hard chrome on hydraulic piston rods and cylinders. With four employees and once again help from friends, the company carved its own niche in the plating industry.

In Texas, during my college years, I raised and trained Appaloosa horses; I tamed colts to get them ready for sale. My horses were National Grand Champions for three consecutive years. Today I apply my teaching, training and business expertise in my role as a Dale Carnegie instructor and sales representative in Silicon Valley—teaching others to be successful by taking charge of their lives and developing their enormous potentials.

One of the highlights of my life was in 1985 when three generations of my family flew across the country from California to Oshkosh, Wisconsin, to the "National Experimental Aircraft Association Fly-In." My two home-built planes made the trip: My seventy-five-year-old mother, Onilla Boling, and I flew my biplane; and my nineteen-year-old son, Willie Turner, flew the Fly Baby, then painted red. He refused to fly mom's "Pink" plane. We were featured on the front page of *USA Today* and the *Evening Magazine* television program.

It was a quest where I learned to respect the skills and decision-making abilities of my son Willie and came to admire my mother even more for her spirit of adventure. There were no "Generation Gaps"—only the wind beneath our wings.

When you plan a cross-country trip by air you fly "one leg at a time"—from Point A to B, B to C, and so on. I have used that concept for my own personal planning. Compartmentalize your tasks and do them one step at a time.

I have faced many challenges as a pilot and the passion for what I was experiencing helped me through the tough times. I've been lost and scared, tired and discouraged, doubting and critical—but deep in my heart was the passion and desire to live life as an adventure. Get turned on to "life" and "life" will turn on to you.

With perseverance and tenacity you can make your wishes a reality. Follow these concepts for your continued success: visualize, believe in yourself, keep hold of your dream, ask for help, share your passion, and maintain a positive attitude toward risk and adventure.

In summary, difficulties will happen. My mother raised me to believe that I can do anything I set my mind to doing. She also said I was responsible for what my mind was thinking. And if I wasn't getting the results I wanted, I had better check my thinking.

Planning the Rest of your Life

Examine Your Thinking: Have a brainstorming session with yourself. What opportunities, challenges and experiences still lie ahead for you? Ask yourself the following questions and list your answers.

☐ What do I want to do with the rest of my life? What would I do if I could not fail? Keep an open mind and name a few things.

☐ What do I want to experience?

☐ What do I want to see?

☐ What do I want to learn?

☐ What do I want to change and leave better than I found it?

☐ What do I want to do for the people who are important to me?

☐ Now that you know what you are going to do for the rest of your life, share your excitement and make it happen one step at a time.

Chapter 13
Hold On to
Your Dream

"Get a clear mental picture of what you want,
infuse it with emotion, and hold on to it"

—

Skip Ross[11]

with Don "atomicboy" Kruse

WHEN *Don was nine years old he closed his first major deal: He persuaded his dad to let him use his dad's cherished Leica camera to take photos while they were walking in picturesque Hilo, Hawaii. Don had never used the Leica before but many times had watched his father use it—and now Don wanted to do it. When the film was processed a few weeks later, those first photos of Don's were better than the pictures his father took!*

Thus began Don's love affair with photography. Growing up, he almost always had a camera by his side ready to take photos whenever he saw something that sparked his interest. In the years that followed, photography became his first love and ambition.

✳   ✳   ✳

I had a solid vision several years ago. I envisioned owning a digital photo printing service—a complete, high-quality digital photo business where customers could wait for their prints in the plush waiting room while drinking a cup of espresso and looking at beautiful photo frames, albums and other quality merchandise in which to display their photos.

My dream began in 1990 when I was in my mid-twenties. I had been promoted to manager of the largest camera shop in Berkeley at that time. I had the opportunity to learn both the good and the bad sides of management. I discovered I could easily figure out how to cut costs, identify and eliminate low-selling products, and evaluate and recommend a computer system for the store; if the computer system were purchased, it would have paid for itself in one year by reducing inventory overhead and sales errors. As manager, I also developed and honed my budgeting and financial planning skills.

I had keen marketing ideas that included getting Kodak to park their NASCAR racing car outside the store for one day. It caused such a traffic jam, as cars slowed down to admire it, that the police wanted the car removed. But I had acquired a one-day city permit, so the car remained parked where it was for that memorable and exciting day. Many new customers came to the store frequently for many months thereafter due to the impression the racing car made on them.

The negative side was that the owner didn't seem interested in building the business and the bookkeepers seemed to revise the monthly profit and loss figures hourly depending on the system they were using at the time. Primarily, the owner didn't seem to care. By early 1992, customers were asking for digital photo printing. I was enthusiastic about this new innovation and researched the process extensively—I could see that it could be profitable for the camera shop. The owner wasn't interested, however, and did not want to invest any money in it.

So one day in 1992, at age 29, I decided to make a positive change in my life. I quit the camera shop and proceeded to find a business partner and begin planning to open the first digital photo printing store in Northern California. We decided that Berkeley was the best location for our first store because we were familiar with the customers there. I persuaded Kodak to give us equipment in advance of the first payment to get us started—the brand new Apple Power Macintosh computers, digital photo printers, as well as other equipment, supplies and paper.

The first lesson I learned is that "you have to have a good credit history to get a loan for the business." But, I didn't have that. For the first time I realized I had to clean up my act and pay my bills on time. Before the business ever opened, the partnership dissolved for various reasons, including the difficulty of obtaining a loan.

On a more positive note, I learned the value of networking. While I was looking for a loan, someone gave me the name of a lawyer who specialized in real estate development. He was impressed with our concept of a digital photo printing business and said he would keep me in mind if he could find some investors for our business. Months later, after the partnership folded, the lawyer contacted me. All of my extensive knowledge of the digital photo printing business paid off. The lawyer put me in contact with someone in Southern California who wanted to start a digital photo printing business. I became a consultant and provided the Southern California entrepreneur with the information he needed to start his own business.

Since that time I have been on the high-tech, Internet path: first, working for a major Web-development company and then working for the fastest-growing magazine publisher both in print and on the World Wide Web.

Today I am doing what I want to do. I quit a comfortable job to do what I enjoy and for a time it was a struggle. I built my credit; I have stock options; and best of all, I have the love of my life, my new bride, Carli.

I still have my aspiration to own the best customer-oriented digital photo-printing store in the country. To hold on to that ambition I own the Web domain for **atomicFOTO.com**. I aim to bring that dream to fruition.

Renewing Your Dream

Sometimes a person has an aspiration that they have to put on hold just like Don did.

☐ Can you think of a wish you put on hold?

_____

_____

_____

☐ Are you ready to rekindle it? _____

☐ How have you been keeping it alive?

_____

_____

_____

☐ Next, write down some small steps that you can take to rekindle the vision.

- Perhaps the step you want to take is to network and tell others about your dream. People will give you names or refer you to others if they believe in you and trust you. You must promise yourself that you will contact every lead you get. Maybe you will want to write a business plan to help you get started.

- Write your small steps below:

_____

_____

_____

_____

_____

☐ Finally write one major step you will have to take. This usually will oust you out of your comfort zone. Allow yourself to take this step although it may be challenging. Identify someone who has already accomplished this, and call them. Ask for help—something wonderful might happen.

_____

_____

_____

_____

Do you have a clear mental picture of your dream? Do you feel passion when you visualize it? If you answered yes, then hold on to that vision and enjoy the journey along the way there.

Chapter 14
Follow Your
Bliss

"If you want to be happy,
you have to get up every morning
and forget the past."
—

Doug Jones

with Doug Jones

ON April Fools Day in 1990 with $600 Doug Jones started his company, Mortgage Magic, in San Jose, on a spiritual impulse. Today Mortgage Magic is a multimillion-dollar company in Silicon Valley with thirty-seven employees.

One day Doug Jones sent me an e-mail message that read, "Have a great day. I am so happy. I just want to pass it on." That was all he wrote. Enjoying life and having fun are all integral to Doug Jones's philosophy for a content, healthy and successful life. Doug's entrepreneurial spirit inspires and impacts his employees. He shares the fullness of his human qualities and clear vision with his staff—conveying enthusiasm, high energy and conviction. He delegates well, encouraging his employees' independence from daily direction. Another way Doug uses his expansive energy is in giving back to the community.

✳ ✳ ✳

WITH more than thirty years of banking experience, I began my mortgage company on a spiritual impulse. At church one Sunday, the pastor gave a sermon called "Follow Your Bliss." I was so inspired by this message that I quit my finance job the next day and went about creating Mortgage Magic. Then doubt crept in, so I went back to church the next Sunday, and the message again assured me that I had done the right thing.

Mortgage Magic gradually led me down three additional follow-your-bliss avenues : 1) Sales Magic—a sales training program I introduced for employees and the public, 2) professional speaking, with more than a hundred engagements a year, and 3) presenting shows as a magician.

My own life illustrates the power of visioning and faith. I was raised in the Great Dismal Swamp, at the corner of North Carolina and Virginia. My family was so poor that I rarely wore shoes, and at the age of ten I was sent to an orphanage where they measured my IQ at 95. I graduated at the bottom 25 percent of my high school class.

When I was 21, I visited the home of a customer who greatly impressed me. He had the Dale Carnegie certificate hanging on his wall. I was so shy and backward--a real "country bumpkin", that when I started college I had to take "bonehead" English. Finishing college took "forever." I knew I wanted to be successful but did not know how. Formal education was very difficult for me. I had already had a baby at 20 and had to work. I knew my path would be difficult. I wanted to take that Dale Carnegie course, but did not have any extra money, so I had to finance the course. I obtained a loan through Avco Financial Services.

The Dale Carnegie Sales Course changed my life: The program gave me the self-confidence I needed to begin my career; and, it taught me how to be a friendly, positive and caring person. After I completed the course, I took a job with the finance company that had given me the loan to take The Dale Carnegie Course. That was the beginning of my career in finance.

Because of my background, I have incorporated a philosophy of community service into my company. Employees are expected to give back to the community. When I was 7 years old and in a children's home, I remember the Salvation Army bringing food, toys and a tree at Christmas. It made me feel great and accepted in society. All my life people have helped me, and I wanted to do the same.

Today, my staff and I walk the extra mile. We pay our bills and contribute to the community. The community awards our company has received over the years are my proudest treasures. Among these awards is The Community Excellence Award from the San Jose Chamber and TCI Cablevision for our work. Other awards were the ARIS Project, YWCA, Crippled Children's Society, YMCA, Boy and Girl Scouts, Tapestry and Talent. We painted a disabled customer's home. We have driven the blind, shopped with kids, and read to the elderly. We have also raised money for charities. I swam from Alcatraz to San Francisco for a personal fund raiser. I have also raised money in walks and 10K races. We have a fundraiser every year to support AIDS Hospice Hospital in Thailand. Every year since 1998, one of our employees has actually paid for the two directors/workers to visit the United States each Christmas. While they are here, she puts on the fundraiser.

I feel it is my duty to use all of my God-given talents according to Matt. 25:35-40, the verses in which the Lord praises his believers who have used their talents to help others. I motivate and empower my employees to handle the daily business of the office. And, a resulting benefit is that I can spend more time working on the projects that I love to do. Helping other people is more important to me than making money—we remember Socrates and his philosophical words, but we forget the names of most rich people.

At Mortgage Magic we go on a yearly planning retreat to the beautiful Monterey area by the Pacific Ocean. With our yellow pads in hand, we talk and dream. We keep talking and establish some "I wish" goals. Later we type up the goals and the intentions begin to work on their own. We visualize what we want and imagine it in place.

Our company is the luckiest in the world! After visualizing what we needed for our new offices, another company heard about our aims. They gave us almost everything we needed and requested: office furniture, two moving vans and thirteen men to help move the furniture to the new offices—all for *free*. We only needed to purchase the computers.

Life is meant to be fun and to be enjoyed. We deserve to love our work and have fun with our loved ones and friends. I encourage everyone to give back to the community, enjoy life to the fullest, enjoy your work, have fun with your coworkers, family and friends, and you will experience the entrepreneurial spirit.

Goal Setting in the Park

Why not try Doug's goal-setting method for yourself: "Visualize it, write it down, and the goal takes on a life of its own," Doug says. Now it is your turn to *do* it. Plan to spend the day on this activity.

☐ Go to your local park or any other quiet place you love.

☐ Bring a yellow pad or journal and a pen, or a laptop, and bring any thing else you need.

☐ Visualize and begin writing your goals. Write whatever comes to your mind—you can always revise it later if you wish.

☐ Stay as long as you want. You might want to pack a picnic lunch and bring a radio. Enjoy yourself with this activity.

☐ Leave when you feel your list is complete.

☐ Type up your list (if you haven't already done so) and print it.

☐ Post it where you can see it every day—read each goal daily.

☐ *Believe it.* Believe it is going to happen.

☐ Finally, *do it* one step at a time. Prioritize your objectives. Select the first goal you want to achieve. Assign yourself tasks (steps) that will take you to your goal, and begin with the first step. Only you can make it happen.

If you prefer, do your goal setting with someone else; this can reinforce your commitment to your ambitions because you have shared it with someone else. Remember to communicate your needs to your friends and colleagues when appropriate; they might know a person or resource that can help you achieve some of your goals.

To help you with this visualization exercise, imagine what it would feel like to reach your aims. Would you smile more? Walk with confidence? Enjoy life more? Have more peace of mind? Most important: just like Doug's group, *have fun* with this exercise.

Chapter 15
Unleash Your
Creativity

"When you receive inspiration,
write it down!"
—
Napoleon Hill

with Sal Dossani

FROM computer consultant to president of a travel agency and storyteller, Sal Dossani epitomizes imagination and inspiration. Sal came to the United States in 1975 as a college student from Pakistan. He tried many different occupations but nothing satisfied his need to contribute to his life in a meaningful manner. Recently he decided that he needs to do work that fulfills his heart's desires. In his search, he discovered a communication program that is fulfilling his need to help others: a program where he can use his insights and creativity.

Sal is a storyteller. He loves to tell stories where a lesson can be applied to life. Here's one of his delightful stories:

✳   ✳   ✳

ONCE UPON A TIME, there lived a young man of great wealth and resources, whose father had bequeathed 3 things to him: a sword, a talking parrot and a silver chalice. He lived a life of great ease and comfort. In the mornings he'd wake up and head out to the beach to meditate. Come midday, he'd have a sumptuous meal of pheasant, venison and other choice meats, topped off with fruits of great rarity and exquisite taste. In the evenings, he'd go off to the theater and enjoy a night of entertainment and refinement.

In this manner, he lived for many days and even more nights. But inevitably, as is the way of things, he grew tired of the unvarying nature of his delights and decided that he'd like to explore life and all the various possibilities it had in store for him.

So, one day, without saying a word to anyone, he saddled his horse and set off to discover what lay in store for him. He rode and he rode and he rode, and then...he rode some more. Soon night fell, and finding himself far from human habitation, he tethered his horse under a tree and lay down to sleep beside it.

Morning came. He woke, went to the nearby stream, splashed his face with water, took some food out of his saddlebags and ate. Feeling refreshed and full of life, he continued his journey.

Soon he came to a land where a dragon was terrorizing the people. When the inhabitants saw this tall, strong and handsome young man, they came out and begged him for help. Quicker than the blink of an eye, he took out his sword and killed the dragon. The people were overjoyed. They offered the kingship of their land to him, but he said he needed to continue his journey. They begged him to come back and become their king, once his journey was over. He promised to think about it.

After many more adventures of a similar and dissimilar kind, the young man came to another country. In this land, there lived a princess, who could never stop crying because she was so sad. The king had proclaimed that whoever could make her laugh would win her hand in marriage and become the future ruler of the land. People from miles around came and told jokes, made funny faces and even stood on their heads, but nothing could make the princess laugh. Upon hearing of the ailment of the princess, the young man immediately went to her with his talking parrot. The parrot started telling her stories, jokes and anecdotes of the most amusing kind. First the princess stopped crying. Then she started smiling and then she began to laugh. Peals and peals of laughter rang out amidst the solemn hallways of the king's court. The king was amazed. He offered the young man the princess' hand and the kingdom, but our hero promised to think about it and to give his answer when his journey was over.

As he continued on, he came to a land where almost everyone had become mad through drinking water from a polluted river. A wise man had forecast that someone would come by one day and take a sip of that water by scooping it up in a silver chalice, and when that would happen, the river would become unpolluted again and everyone would become sane again.

Upon reaching that land, the young man, as was his custom, took out his silver chalice and drank the water. Sooner than it takes to tell, the river reverted back to its former purity and the people rubbed their eyes and awoke, as if from a deep, deep sleep. When they realized what had happened, they offered him the rulership of their kingdom. He politely declined and continued on.

A few days later, he recalled his father's words, "My son, when you have used the resources I have given you, for the benefit of others, your journey will be complete," and realized his lesser journey was over and the greater one was about to begin.

By this time, the young man had become wiser and more confident and realized that he had the choice of ruling over any one of three kingdoms. He chose the middle one, in which the princess lived. They were married amongst much merriment and fanfare.

Thus the young man, who became a prince, and his princess spent their lives in happiness and contentment, till, in the fullness of time, they became the rightful rulers of one of the most prosperous and happy kingdoms the world has ever seen.

The Young Man Who Became a Prince, ©2000 by Sal Dossani (Used with permission)

L IFE can be a wonderful adventure and we should persist in our quest to achieve our deepest wishes, much like the prince did in the story above. We need to understand our human character: As we live our lives, we contribute to the lives of others, and in doing so our identity and our self-knowledge evolves. Assisting others helps make our own lives richer and more fulfilling.

I heard about Neuro Linguistic Programming (NLP) and began taking classes in this communication program. NLP, as taught at NLP Marin (California), allows people to rediscover their human potential and heritage. We are born with a heritage, an inheritance, that we can either change, build up, or let slip away.

With NLP training, I am learning the foundations of communication and change. I am opening a whole new world for myself, as I break old behaviorial patterns and integrate new life changing behaviors that will enable me to change and grow. I am deepening my interpersonal communication skills so that I can understand and work well with others.

Learning is a lifelong experience. Without knowledge, you cannot understand yourself. Without understanding yourself, you cannot understand life. And if you don't understand life, you certainly won't be happy.

At a recent NLP training, I expressed my life dreams: "To live life with a complete choice of freedom—freedom in the sense of not being ruled by inner desires or outer influences. Choice in the sense of not being hampered by any obstacle." Freedom is essential for every human being, because without it one leads a dull and dreary life, like that of an automaton; whilst, with freedom, one can begin to live like a true human being.

Success is always a journey. Once we actualize a dream, in time we want to move on to something else that will challenge and fulfill our lives. Be creative and use your inspiration and imagination to follow your dreams.

Activity

Unleashing Creativity

☐ Write a creative, imaginary story just like Sal did. Let your creative juices flow. Focus on telling the story. Keep on writing and writing until the story is complete. You will feel a sense of accomplishment when you have finished your story.

☐ Now use those creative-writing skills to write down your goals and dreams. Use your imagination and inspiration. Staying positive and believing in yourself are the first steps to success.
Have a happy journey.

Acknowledgements

Thanks
to all the book contributors
for sharing their personal stories with me
for inclusion in this book.
I have learned so much from them.
They are indeed **Silicon Valley Dynamos**.

A deep appreciation for the support, ideas and
encouragement that I received from my favorite mentors:
Alan Weiss, *Carlos Figueroa*, and *Florence Littauer*.
They truly are winners.

Some fantastic ideas and suggestions came from my book
reviewers *whom I thank from the bottom of my heart*
for their honest, gutsy opinions:
Cathy Gallagher, *Dawn Fry*, and *Teri Coleman*.

I want to acknowledge all the publishing professionals
for their commitment to creativity and excellence.
My thanks to:
Production Managers: *Simon Warwick-Smith* and *Patty Vadinsky*
Illustrations: *Jim Hunt*
Cover/Interior Design: *Robb Pawlak / Pawlak Design*
Editor: *Netty Kahan*
Photographer: *Bill Martinelli*

Contributors

1. *Carlos Figueroa* is a Sales and Self-Improvement Trainer. Today he is a Master Mentor as he continues to guide and encourage hundreds of people in their quest for success. Always challenging himself, Carlos, at 60-something, has returned to college. He has been married to Ileana for 38 years. He has a son and two daughters.

2. *Nancy Kruse* currently is a Director for the top-rated animated television series, *The Simpsons*; rated the best show of the 20th Century by *Time Millennium*[12]. She joined *The Simpsons* during the first season and has been with it ever since. She began in the entry-level position of Background Clean-up Artist and has worked her way up through most of the production capacities including Background Layout Artist, Character Layout Artist, Assistant Director and Storyboarding. Nancy is famous for designing the corn pattern curtains in the Simpsons' kitchen and for misspelling the word "Pageant" prominently in a background of the premiere episode.

3. *Michael James* works as a Photographer/Editor for WSTM-TV in Syracuse, New York. The former San Francisco Bay Area resident is happily married to his wife, Kelly, for two years. He spends his spare time on .writing projects. He currently is working on a screenplay for Film or Television entitled, "All I Ever Wanted..."

4. *Debbie Murray* is Vice President of Customer Care for BulaBay Corporation. Her career has encompassed a wide range of responsibilities in the public and private sectors, as a consultant and as an employee, which has included development, documentation, training, project management, and systems analysis. She was a Senior Director of CAI's Professional Services Organization. Her responsibilities included management of an international staff of branch managers, team managers, integration design analysts, integration engineers and consultants. She enjoys walking on the beach, creative writing, and drawing and painting. She has two children and three grandchildren. She studied chemistry, Physics, Computer Science and Social Science at Westminster College (Salt Lake City, UT), and was a recipient of

the Phi Eta Sigma Scholastic Achievement Award and three-time recipient of the Earl W. Stouffer Scholarship.

5. *Loc Van Phan* is a Senior Electronics Test Engineer in Silicon Valley working for a new startup company, GuideTech Inc. His hobbies are soft rock, playing guitar, audio video gear, computer, watching sports and the beach.

6. *Dr. Chao Huang*—Internet entrepreneur, President and CEO of Joymail.com: an Internet and e-mail services company that he founded in 1998. He previously served with various high-tech companies in positions as, International Consultant, Program Manager, and Senior Staff Engineer and Senior Staff Scientist. He has achieved five degrees in a nine-year period that includes B.S.E.E., M.S Electrical Engineering, M.S Civil Engineering, M.S. Mathematics, and Ph.D. Computer Engineering. He is also the founder of Szechuan Garden Restaurant, Anova Microsystems Inc., ID Star Inc., and ecChannels Inc. He has been awarded one patent with Lockheed and four others are pending. His articles on "Digital Signal Processing, Speech and Image Processing" have been published in more than 30 Technical publications. His community services included Trustee of the Mountain View City Library, and Director of the Pacific Neighbors: San Jose-Tainan (Taiwan) Sister City Committee.

7. *Dave Latner*, A native of California and the Bay Area, Dave now lives in San Francisco and still regards himself as a tourist, "because tourists have more fun". When he is not exploring the nooks and crannies of the city, Dave freelances in marketing and business consulting. He is a member of the board of directors for the Eureka theatre, a San Francisco theatre company dedicated to producing thought provoking and socially conscious stage plays. A book on his travels is in the works.

8. *Joan Clout-Kruse*, speaker, trainer, author and founder of CloutPower!, a training company (**www.cloutpower.com**) focused on personal effectiveness and embracing change. A native San Franciscan, she has been a working mother in the business world for Corporate America companies for more than 30 years and eight years as a business owner. She has been married to Don M. for 38 years and has three grown children;

Debbie, Don A., and Nancy; two grandchildren, and three great grandchildren. She has presented Communication Training programs to youth in her community, including youth-at-risk at the county juvenile detention facility. Joan is a founding member of Success Builders International™, A Personal Development Organization founded in Silicon Valley in the year 2000. On a sunny day you can see her inline skating on the streets of Foster City.

9. *Marc Isaac Potter*, Listening Coach™, helps people improve their listening skills. He has volunteered, and presented his seminars at Edison McNair Academy, a middle school; and Alliance for Community Care that helps people with mental health challenges. Marc's poetry has appeared in *Firelands Review* (Bowling Green State University), WPA (a project of the City of Palo Alto) and *two steps in*, a journal of the arts.

10. *Kilsoon Kim*, a budding opera singer in North Korea, lost her parents and siblings during the Korean conflict in the late '40s. She fled to South Korea and taught music, singing and piano in local elementary schools. Today, her daughter *Jinsoo Terry* is the Director of Manufacturing for Cut Loose, a clothing manufacturer in San Francisco. Jinsoo has a Master's Degree in engineering from Pusan National University in Pusan, South Korea and is well known as an expert in garment dyeing.

11. *Cesar Plata* founded **www.muybueno.net** in September 1998 in Silicon Valley. Muybueno.net aims to inform and unite the Bay Area Latino Community by promoting Business, Community, Culture, and Education. Prior to this venture, Cesar held technical marketing engineering / manufacturing roles at various Silicon Valley semiconductor equipment companies. He holds a B.S. in Mechanical Engineering from the University of California, Davis.

12. *Gail Turner*, Vice President of Corporate Solutions for Dale Carnegie Training, loves to talk to people. This is a fortunate passion as a professional speaker and trainer. Gail has presented to and trained groups of 5 to 4,000 in Leadership, Time Management, Communication, and Human Relations Development. Gail's hobbies are as varied and exciting as her story. They include building and flying experimental airplanes, and riding her flashy new teal and silver 800 Kawasaki Vulcan Classic motorcycle. Gail also loves her Arabian horse, Strutter, and takes him on trail rides in the Sierras. She has successfully owned and operated an electroplating plant, manufacturing hydraulic piston rods, the only one of its kind on the West Coast. She is the first woman to build and fly her own airplane across the country.

13. Self-taught *Don "atomicboy" Kruse* (**www.atomicboy.com**) learned photography, filmmaking, videomaking, web development and design, systems administration and networking, various computer operating systems—Windows®, Mac OS, LINUX—on his own. His love for the high-tech field has led him to work for such companies as Organic, a major web development company (**www.organic.com**) and The Future Networks, a high-tech magazine publisher (**www.imaginemedia.com**).

14. *Doug Jones* is the founder and CEO of Mortgage Magic; a San Jose based Mortgage Company. His other areas of interest are motivational speaking, sales training, magic, and charity work. He serves on the board of the Salvation Army in Santa Clara County and performs free magic shows each year for local churches, schools, and nonprofit organizations. His sports activities include swimming from Alcatraz to San Francisco and competing in the longest recorded tug-of-war. He has been married to Trudy for 33 years and has two grown children.

15. *Sal Dossani* came from Pakistan to the U. S. in 1975 to study Electrical Engineering. Over the past twenty years he has had a variety of careers ranging from finance to computer programming to business consultancy. In 1991 he purchased a travel agency and has been in that business ever since. Sal is affiliated with various organizations, such as the Institute for the Study of Human Knowledge, Institute of Noetic Sciences, Future Watch Society, the Commonwealth Club, Neuro Linguistics Program in Marin, the Sierra Club, Toastmasters, and Success Builders International. He is a storyteller, and helps people in interpreting their dreams.

Footnotes

1   *The Circle of Innovation*, Tom Peters, Vintage Books, 1999, p. 185.

2   *Getting Unstuck*, Dr. Sidney Simon, Warner Books, 1988, p. 253.

3   *Thank You Very Much*, Holly Stiel, Ten Speed Press, 1995, p. 53.

4   "Why Don't I Do What I Know I Should Do"? *How to Master the Art of Selling*, Tom Hopkins, 1982, Warner Books, p.68.

5   Daniel Goleman, author of Emotional Intelligence, "where excellence becomes effortless, crowd and competitors disappearing into a blissful, steady absorption in the moment", describes "The Zone".

6   Napoleon Hill and W. Clement Stone, *Success Through a Positive Mental Attitude*, ©1987, p. 119, Pocketbooks, New York.

7   Daniel Goleman, *ibid.*

8   *U.S. News & World Report*, "How Shy Is Too Shy?" by Joannie M. Schrof & Stacey Schultz, 6/21/99.

9   *Ibid.*

10 "Overcoming Shyness," ©2000 Nancy Wesson, Ph.D. Web site **www.wespsych.com**, 11/5/00

11 *Say Yes to your Potential*, Skip Ross with Carole C. Carlson, Word, Inc., 1983, p.83

12 *Time Millennium Collector's Edition*, December 31, 1999, *The Simpsons* rated best show of the century, p. 42.

About
the
Author

WITH more than 30 years of experience in Corporate America, including management positions at Stanford University and UC-Berkeley, Joan Clout-Kruse knows the challenges facing management and working professionals. She is a member of the Institute of Certified Professional Managers, and since 1987 holds the Certified Administrative Manager designation, demonstrating her continued commitment of the business world. She resides in Foster City, California.

For up-to-date information on Silicon Valley Dynamos check our website: **www.siliconvalleydynamos.com**

Order Form

Top 10 Traits *of*

Silicon Valley

Dynamos

*Inspiring Stories and Great Ideas for
Achieving Success in Your Life*

Joan Clout-Kruse

Please send *Top 10 Traits of Silicon Valley Dynamos* to:

Name (please print): _____

Address: _____

_____

City: _____ State: _____ Zip: _____

Country: _____

_____ Book(s) at $12.95 each $ _____

California residents add 7.25% sales tax. $ _____

Add $2.00 shipping and handling for the first book
and $1.00 for each additional book. $ _____

TOTAL ENCLOSED $ _____

Mail your check payable to:

Dunhill Publishing   18340 Sonoma Hwy   Sonoma, CA 95476

ONLINE ORDERS: You can also order this book from AMAZON.COM